COLLEGE LIBRARY

**Please return this book by the date stamped below
- if recalled, the loan is reduced to 10 days**

Fines are payable for late return

Everyday Communication: Case Studies of Behavior in Context
Wendy Leeds-Hurwitz & Stuart J. Sigman, Series Editors

Smooth Talkers: The Linguistic Performance of Auctioneers and Sportscasters
Koenraad Kuiper

In Search of a Voice: Karaoke and the Construction of Identity in Chinese America
Casey Man Kong Lum

Confrontation Talk: Arguments, Asymmetries, and Power on Talk Radio
Ian Hutchby

Conversations About Illness: Family Preoccupations With Bulimia
Wayne A. Beach

The Fragile Community: Living Together With AIDS
Mara B. Adelman and Lawrence R. Frey

Puerto Rican Discourse: A Sociolinguistic Study of a New York Suburb
Lourdes Torres

Puerto Rican Discourse: A Sociolinguistic Study of a New York Suburb

Lourdes Torres
University of Kentucky

LEA LAWRENCE ERLBAUM ASSOCIATES, PUBLISHERS
1997 Mahwah, New Jersey

Lawrence Erlbaum Associates, Inc., Publishers
10 Industrial Avenue
Mahwah, New Jersey 07430

Cover design by Mairav Salomon-Dekel

Library of Congress Cataloging-in-Publication Data

Torres, Lourdes, 1959–
Puerto Rican discourse : a sociolinguistic study of a
New York suburb / Lourdes Torres.
     p. cm.
    Includes bibliographical references and index.
    ISBN 0-8058-1930-4 (cloth : alk. paper). —
ISBN 0-8058-1931-2 (pbk. : alk. paper)
    1. Sociolinguistics — New York (State) —
Brentwood. 2. Puerto Ricans — New York (State)
— Brentwood — Languages. I. Title.
    P40.45.U5T67 1997
    306.4'4'09747245—dc20   96–46361
                                  CIP

Printed in the United States of America
10 9 8 7 6 5 4 3 2 1

Contents

Editors' Preface

Interdisciplinary scholarship generally develops from the recognition of a previously unexamined (or underexamined) problem or from recognition of the difficulties in studying some topic from within the confines of a single discipline's theory and methodology. Such is the case with sociolinguistics, which, at its best, combines insights into broad patterns of communal life (including a sensitivity to race or ethnicity, gender, class, and economic issues) with detailed analyses of language structure and use. It is just such a project which forms the basis for Lourdes Torres' *Puerto Rican Discourse: A Sociolinguistic Study of a New York Suburb,* the sixth volume in Lawrence Erlbaum Associates' Everyday Communication series.

We are especially pleased to include Torres' work in the series because it introduces this linguist to a new audience of anthropologists, communication scholars, English as a second language (ESL) educators, narratologists, and sociologists, as well as those in (socio)linguistics already familiar with her work. Torres is bilingual and a Latina and was thus in a unique position to study the relationship between community values, structures, and language performance among Puerto Ricans living in a New York City suburb.

To study the complex interweaving of social, cultural, and linguistic elements in Brentwood, NY, Torres made use of multiple methods. First, she positioned herself as a participant-observer in the various public venues she could access: street festivals, public hearings, cafes, and so on. Second, she administered a language attitude questionnaire to 350 members of the community (including children as well as adults). Third, she conducted qualitative interviews with 30 informants, on each occasion eliciting narratives about their migration experiences, xenophobia from their neighbors, self-hatred resulting from the adoption of the majority group's linguistic symbols and values, and the sexism and violence in the community itself. Taken together, these various data sets constitute a corpus that permits the researcher to examine the similarities and differences in the social experiences and linguistic behavior of three types of community members—first-generation immigrants to North America whose primary language is Spanish; their second-generation children who were primarily educated in New York and have varying bilingual competencies; and their third-generation grandchildren, for whom English is the dominant (although not exclusive) means of expression.

One of the first myths dispelled by Torres' meticulous attention to her data is the presumed similarity of Hispanic and Latino communities across the United States. Her research establishes important contrasts with previous reports of Mexican Americans in Los Angeles and Texas, for example. Attitudes toward Spanish and English, and competency with various grammatical features of both languages, are not uniform across Hispanic and Latino communities.

Second, Torres contributes to our understanding of linguistic creativity among bilinguals and of feature loss. Her analysis reveals that monolingual Spanish, monolingual English, and bilingual speakers all access the same grammatical and rhetorical repertoire in producing their narratives. Although there is some loss of Spanish among the latter two groups, the decline of particular grammatical features is not always linear. Also, all three groups creatively employ English phrases and syntactic constructions in producing their Spanish narratives.

Third, Torres contextualizes the unique sociological features of the Brentwood community and its members' linguistic practices by examining significant themes in speakers' narratives. Not only does she show how code-switching is used for rhetorical purposes, she also reveals the complex relationship between key themes related to living in the community—internalized racism and ethnocentrism, for example—and the linguistic devices available for conveying these in English and Spanish.

What does all of this reveal about the relationship between communication and context, a primary theme of this monograph series? Simply put, Torres' study reminds us that any hopes of approaching a sophisticated understanding of that relationship will need to confront the complexity of both objects of study, that is, both communication and context. Her study reveals that even one communication channel, the linguistic, must be studied for both its structural and discursive patterning, as one code among many, and both synchronically and diachronically. The research also reveals that, in attempting to frame an entire community as one's context of investigation, one must be prepared to observe broad patterns of behavior, including media depictions of the community's struggles, as well as private reflections on aspirations, goals, and these struggles. These various data sources permit the researcher to construct the jigsaw pattern of the community's behavior.

We appreciate Lourdes Torres' efforts in this regard and the valuable insights into the Brentwood Puerto Rican community her study provides.

Wendy Leeds-Hurwitz
Stuart J. Sigman

Acknowledgments

Many people have facilitated the completion of this book. At SUNY Stony Brook, Alicia Geli, Vilma Concha, Liliana Paredes, and Lou Deutsch helped me prepare, distribute, and collect surveys at the various schools in Brentwood. At the University of Kentucky, Mary Daniels, Michele Barosh, and Kristi Hislope read and commented on drafts of chapters. Special thanks go to Ann Russo, who read many versions of this book and provided inspiring comments as well as constant support.

I am especially indebted to the editors of this series, Wendy Leeds-Hurwitz and Stuart J. Sigman; both offered stimulating feedback and advice throughout the preparation of this text.

Finally, I would like to thank the Puerto Rican community of Brentwood who took me into their homes and shared their lives with me. I dedicate this book to them.

Introduction

In *Borderlands / La Frontera*, Gloria Anzaldúa writes, *"Deslenguados. Somos los del español deficiente.* [Tongueless. We are those with deficient Spanish.] We are your linguistic nightmare, your linguistic aberration, your linguistic *mestisaje* [mixture], the subject of your *burla* [mocking]. Because we speak with tongues of fire we are culturally crucified. Racially, culturally and linguistically *somos huérfanos*—we speak an orphan tongue" (Anzaldúa, 1987, p. 58). Anzaldúa underscores the intimate relationship between language and culture; she recognizes the fact that negative assessments made about the language of the Chicano community are associated with other forms of oppression. This reality captures the inescapable links between Latino language and social life.

According to the 1990 census, 22.35 million residents of the United States are of Latino[1] origin; this means that about 1 out of every 11 United States citizens is Latino. Hispanics are the youngest and fastest growing constituents of the United States. The Latino population is expected to double in 30 years and triple in 60 years.[2] The Census Bureau (1991) projects that in the year 2010, Hispanics will surpass Blacks as the largest minority group. Given the increasing importance of Latino communities in the United States and contemporary debates about ethnic language and education, sociolinguistic studies of specific communities are essential.

---

[1]I use the terms *Latino* and *Hispanic* interchangeably. I am not taking a position on the debates about appropriate terminology for persons of Spanish-speaking origins in the United States. I agree that it is problematic to lump all persons of Spanish-speaking origin under one umbrella term, be it Latino, Hispanic, or anything else, given different nationalities, as well as race differences and class issues. However, with Padilla (1985), I agree that terms such as Latino or Hispanic can serve as situational ethnic identifiers when the need for panethnic unity arises.

[2]The number of Hispanics in the United states rose from 9.1 million to 14.6 million in the 10-year period of 1970 to 1980; this figure does not include the millions of undocumented immigrants who reside in the United States. From 1980 to 1990, the Hispanic population grew 53%. Half of the growth has come from immigration and the other half from native births. Many peoples of different nationalities are included under the general term *Latino* or *Hispanic.* According to the 1990 census, Mexicans constitute 63% of the Latino population; Puerto Ricans, 11%, Cubans, 5% and other Hispanics, 22%.

Sociolinguistic study aims to link linguistic structure and social practice to present a unified description of a speech community. Only through an analysis of the language spoken, as well as the speakers' attitudes and ideologies, can we hope to fully comprehend the stable, dynamic, and transitional bilingualisms that exist in Spanish-speaking communities in the United States.

This book explores the dynamic sociolinguistic characteristics of a Puerto Rican community in Brentwood, a suburb in Long Island, New York. In chapters 1 and 2 we see that Puerto Rican young people residing in Brentwood are exposed to more English than Spanish and speak much English in a range of situations in the home and with friends. A common assumption held by linguists, given these dynamics, is that the Spanish these young people speak must be impoverished when compared to varieties employed by speakers in a wide range of settings and with an extensive gamut of situations and interlocutors. If the language of those who speak in restricted contexts is compared with some prescriptive norm or even the Spanish of educated monolingual or bilingual speakers, a more simplified variety is expected of the speakers who have received no formal training in Spanish. But this kind of comparison, so common in the scholarship about U.S. Spanish (Lavandera, 1984; Teschner, Bills, & Craddock, 1975), is not the purpose of this work. I approach the study of U.S. Puerto Rican Spanish with the understanding that what I am examining is *not* a corrupted language, but rather a variety that is evolving in a restricted context. My focus is on the home language use of Spanish-dominant, bilingual, and English-dominant Puerto Rican speakers in a suburban community. I compare the Spanish language use of persons with different migration histories and language proficiencies within the same bilingual community rather than with some external norm.

Most studies of U.S. Spanish concern Mexican American Spanish, and generalizations about all U.S. varieties tend to derive from the study of this subgroup. There is a dire need for studies of other U.S. Latino communities for comparison purposes, because although there are commonalities between Latino subgroups, each community experiences its own unique dynamics as well. Puerto Ricans are the second largest Hispanic subgroup overall as well as the dominant Latino community in many parts of the United States, especially in the East Coast; thus, they are an important group to study.

Much of my data consists of Spanish oral narratives, stories told by Puerto Rican participants from three generational groups about past events that they consider noteworthy. The Spanish I am interested in is the informal variety that speakers use to talk with family and friends. Given that Spanish is a restricted code in the lives of many U.S. Puerto Ricans, it is important to learn of the ways in which the restricted input and output of Spanish affect the evolution of the home language. Among other things, this project can provide insight into language loss and simplification that other studies, which compare speech gathered in nonuniform settings or speech gathered in artificial contexts, cannot adequately measure. A focus on oral narratives allows us to make a valid comparison of how speakers from the same community with differing proficiencies in Spanish use this language when producing a specific discourse unit. Narratives are a rich data source that facilitate analysis not only of the grammatical aspects of language use, but also the strategies people use to convey their messages.

Researching the diminishing language skills of succeeding generations has been a primary preoccupation in studies of Spanish in the United States. The interest of such projects, which document language loss in situations of languages in contact and where Spanish is subordinate, is part of a larger quest to understand universal processes of language attrition in a variety of contexts. Many studies conclude that portions of the language system of U.S. Latinos are changing due to less input and restricted use of Spanish; this is assumed to be especially true for second and third generation Spanish speakers. Determining the processes of linguistic evolution in each variety is one challenge before researchers.

Too often, however, such projects seem to turn into an almost single-minded obsession with charting the demise of Spanish (Bills, 1975; Torres, 1991). Because of the preponderance of studies of this nature, a common association made about U.S. Spanish concerns its deficiency or corruption (Teschner et al., 1975). Often, one small aspect of language use is discussed and serves as the basis for generalizations about the entire language system and communication abilities of speakers. Invariably the generalization concerns a deterioration of or deviation from Standard Spanish (Teschner et al., 1975).

This type of generalization is problematic in the U.S. context, where hostility toward Spanish speakers occurs; the constant reports about deficient speech practices help to perpetuate stereotypes about supposedly deficient speakers. When studying issues involving minority languages, it seems especially difficult to escape the implications of such work at the social and political level. Linguists studying minority languages should understand the political and cultural arena in which their work will be interpreted. One might doubt the relevance of a linguistic study for communities; it is probably true that individual studies are rarely influential in national debates about language issues. However, tendencies of the literature certainly play a role in national public debates about issues such as bilingualism, bilingual education, and other language policy issues (Language Policy Task Force [LPTF], 1978, 1980, 1982).

Silva-Corvalán (1989) argues that investigators interested in linguistic change across generations are reluctant to study U.S. dialects because they will be misinterpreted as saying that Spanish is being lost or that the varieties are degenerate. She states that studies such as hers, which focus on simplification in Mexican American Spanish, in no way make predictions about language loss at a societal level; rather, they are studies of speakers at the lower end of the bilingual continuum.

But there are reasons beyond the political for being cautious with deficit theories of Spanish. In *Chicano Discourse* (1983), Rosaura Sánchez criticizes most work on U.S. Spanish varieties for producing "meaningless quantitative studies, giving us proportions and numerous statistics indicating the number of times a particular variant appeared in the speech of one group or another" (Sánchez, 1983, p. 92) but nothing more. These studies focus on U.S. Spanish as a deficient variety. Sánchez calls for an integrative approach to the study of U.S. Spanish varieties where Latino ways of speaking are described comprehensively. She argues that studies should consider factors such as the social stratification of the community being studied, as well as class ideology, nativity, and residence. It is likely that such integrative community studies will yield insights into the complex role played by Spanish in speakers' lives—a role that cannot be understood when only linguistic structure is examined.

There are thus important differences of approach separating linguists. Some scholars are not content to label any difference in bilingual Spanish as a deviation and a sign of simplification; rather, these linguists take a totally different point of departure in which they ground their work in the reality of the bilingual context. Studies such as those by the Language Policy Task Force (1980, 1982), Pousada and Poplack (1981), Sánchez (1983), and Torres (1989, 1990a), seek to emphasize the heterogeneity of varieties of language in the bilingual communities studied. They attempt to highlight the skill and creativity of the Latino bilinguals who use a variety of linguistic strategies to convey their meaning.

These scholars also exhibit a healthy skepticism concerning some linguists' tendency to ascribe all divergences in the language of U.S. Latinos to English influence. This is not a characteristic unique to scholars interested in the varieties of Spanish in the United States; rather, as Mougeon, Beniak, and Volois (1985) point out, the general tendency when studying any minority language in a contact situation is to account for perceived differences in these varieties in terms of interference from a superordinate language.

Very often in discussions of second or third generation Spanish, linguists focus on only one code, ignoring the reality that the bilingual has several codes at her[3] disposal (Teschner et al., 1975; Torres, 1991);

---

[3]To avoid the use of sexist language, I alternate between the feminine and masculine pronouns when pronouns are used generically throughout this book.

thus, endless studies comparing bilingual Spanish with monolingual Spanish varieties are produced. The nativization of Spanish in a U.S. context means that English will continue to be integrated, especially at the lexical level, in the speech of bilinguals. The question of how speakers achieve this integration and accommodate all the codes in their repertoire is complex. One of the areas I focus on in this study is how English is creatively integrated in the Spanish of bilingual speakers.

SPANISH IN THE UNITED STATES— AN INTEGRATED APPROACH

Many of the studies of change in U.S. Spanish can be located in the tradition of studies about language loss and language death (Dorian, 1981; Gal, 1979). These studies focus on languages that are approaching extinction. But the case of Spanish in the United States is very different from most language death situations. In the United States, there is a constant influx of new Spanish monolingual speakers and a growing mass media network (newspapers, magazines, television and radio transmission) in Spanish that helps maintain the language. Also, although Spanish is a minority language in the United States, it enjoys prestige in an international context. When considering language vitality, it is important to distinguish between societal loss of language use and individual loss of language proficiency. In some Spanish-speaking communities, because of incoming speakers and institutional support, Spanish continues to have a strong presence. At the same time, at the individual or family level in succeeding generations, Spanish often becomes more and more restricted in use. However, this pattern may be arrested or even reversed for some speakers (LPTF, 1980, 1982).

At the individual level, as Andersen (1982) points out, one needs to distinguish between language attrition (the loss of proficiency in a language) and incomplete acquisition of a variety. For situations where speakers receive less input than in a monolingual context, Andersen (1982) proposes two assumptions regarding language attrition. First, if a speaker is not exposed to the type and quantity of the input that speakers of the variety have traditionally been exposed to, it is likely that such speakers will not develop the full range of lexical, phonological, and syntactic distinctions of which other speakers avail themselves. The second assumption is that not all linguistic material will be affected equally. Some linguistic attributes (such as forms and constructions acquired early) will be maintained to the very end; other areas of language (such as the lexicon) might be affected rather quickly. There will be a continuum or a hierarchy of linguistic material, from that which is very susceptible to change to that which is highly resistant. Thus, both societal and individual factors must be considered when studying Spanish language vitality in the United States.

This study addresses these issues through an integrated approach. First, I provide an analysis of the societal factors that impact Spanish language use in the Brentwood community (chap. 1). A language use and attitude survey, plus my observations of the community provide a crucial background for the analysis of speech data (chap. 2). Then, I focus on a range of Spanish linguistic attributes appearing in oral narratives. I show how they function in the speech of community members with various acquisition histories, which have resulted in different degrees of Spanish language proficiency (chap. 3). I show that across groups the lexical level of the language is more affected than the grammatical level by a context of reduced Spanish input and use (chap. 4). Finally, I analyze the content of the narratives collected in the study and describe discourse strategies employed by community members to work out issues of internalized racism and sexism (chap. 5).

DATA COLLECTION AND METHODOLOGY
OF PRESENT STUDY

Three methods were employed to determine language use and language attitudes of Puerto Rican speakers in the Brentwood, NY, community. First, I interacted as a neighbor and researcher with the Puerto Rican residents for a period of 3 years, from 1989 to 1991. In addition, beginning the second year of my work in the community, I interviewed 30 adults, ranging in age from 18 to 65. Each audiotaped interview lasted from 1 to 2 hours and produced a number of narratives for analysis. Finally, I distributed a language use and language attitude survey that was completed by 151 students and 220 parents in the Brentwood school district (see chap. 2).

During my first year in the community I observed the community in a number of public and private contexts; I also participated in community activities and got acquainted with Puerto Rican community members (my observations of the community are discussed in chap. 1). I contacted subjects for the oral interviews through my involvement in some community political and social service organizations, such as *Adelante*, Long Island Hispanic Forum, Puerto Rican Women's Congress, La Unión Hispánica, Head Start, and CHALI (Contemporary Hispanic Art on Long Island). I established contacts with Puerto Ricans in these organizations, and they, in turn, introduced me to their family, friends, and social networks.

During my second and third years in the community, I continued these activities and, in addition, I began a series of audiotaped conversations with community persons of different age groups and migration histories. Generally, people were receptive to being interviewed. A few young people initially agreed to an interview and then changed their minds when I mentioned that I would conduct the interview in Spanish. As in many of the Spanish–English bilingual communities in the United States, the speakers in Brentwood share different degrees of passive and active control of the codes in their linguistic repertoire. Most of the Puerto Ricans I met during the years I spent in Brentwood were able to converse in Spanish with me, although this was not the code with which some people were most comfortable.

I indicated to the participants that I was involved in a study of Latino life on Long Island, and all consented to speak to me on tape about this subject. Because community members knew that I was a university teacher and taught courses about language and culture, my interest in interviewing them did not seem out of place. I spoke in Spanish and requested that the interviewees speak to me in Spanish as well. However, most participants alternated between codes to varying degrees throughout the interviews (see chap. 4).

The narratives I analyze in this study are embedded in interviews that focus on the lives and the attitudes of Latino community members. Although my questions followed a predetermined interview schedule, the conversations were generally open-ended, and participants were encouraged to discuss at length whatever subjects interested them. The narratives I collected are stories that recapitulate past events. They either recount a particular experience that involved the narrator or tell about general experiences in their lives.

Most previous studies on U.S. Spanish structure do not look at actual speech, but rather they are based on data gathered through indirect methods such as pen and paper tasks and grammaticality judgement exercises (i.e., Escamilla, 1982; Lantolf, 1983; Teschner et al., 1975). Those studies that are based on elicited speech data often do not compare speakers participating in the same discourse units. The comparison of the appearance or frequency of verb types, for instance, is not reliable if verbs from the same types of discourse are not elicited, because specific verb tenses and moods are associated with specific discourse units. Although investigators mediate against this through the use of the same preconceived interview schedule with all informants, participants ultimately decide which questions are of interest to them, and they elaborate on the issues most relevant to them. These may or may not be the subjects anticipated by the researcher, and speakers many or may not all produce similar discourse units. For these reasons, narratives are an ideal data source. Narratives are a highly structured discourse unit. They are composed of specific components, each of which is associated with specific linguistic properties (Labov & Waletzky, 1967); thus, comparisons made on the basis of oral narrative study are more meaningful and reliable than comparisons made on the basis of other types of speech.

Although there are various ways to define narratives, my definition of the structure of the narrative closely follows Labov's (1972) formulation. Although a narrative of personal experience may be as brief as two sequential clauses, whose meaning would change if the order of the clauses were changed, most narratives are usually more involved. They can consist of the following components: an abstract, orientation, complicating actions, evaluation, resolution, and coda. A brief narrative is presented below (Text 1-A) to demonstrate these components.

Text 1-A [English translation follows]

1)   *una vez se me presentó una oportunidad fabulosa*
2)   *yo había terminado la escuela*
3)   *vi una casa casi destruida*
4)   *y la cojí con poco dinero*
5)   *la compré destruida*
6)   *pero yo soy una persona*
7)   *que le ve lo positivo a la vida*
8)   *poquito a poquito la arreglé*
9)   *una tablita hoy, una ventana manaña*
10) *y al final me mudé*
11) *fue una aventura excitante*

[1)   once a fabulous opportunity presented itself to me
2)   I had finished school
3)   I saw a broken down house
4)   and I got it cheap
5)   I bought it destroyed
6)   but I am a person
7)   that sees the positive in life
8)   little by little I fixed it
9)   a board today, a window tomorrow
10) and finally I moved
11) it was an exciting adventure]

The abstract serves as a brief summary of the narrative to be presented (line 1). An orientation section often establishes the setting, the time, and the participants involved (lines 2–3). The complicating actions are the portions of the narrative where the story unfolds (lines 4–5, 8–9). The evaluation sections, which can be present throughout the narrative, or in a separate section, are where the speaker expresses why the narrative is tellable, why it is interesting, exciting, and worth telling (6–7). The resolution explains what finally happened (line 10), and the coda often serves as a transition from narrative time to the present (line 11).

I chose 60 Spanish narratives of personal experience from the transcripts of the interviews. I selected stories of similar length and topics. I include the narratives of both men and women in my sample. One third of the narratives are taken from the interviews with first generation speakers (Group 1); these persons were born in Puerto Rico and came to New York in their teenage years. They have lived in Brentwood most of their lives and range in age from 40 to 60. These speakers are Spanish-dominant. Group 2 speakers, who produced the second group of narratives, came to New York as small children, before the age of 5, or they were born in New York. They have spent most of their lives on Long Island; these speakers range in age from 30 to 50 and are bilingual. The third group of participants (Group 3) are persons born in Brentwood who were in their late teens or early 20s at the time of the study. Group 3 speakers are English-dominant. Because I was interested in studying language evolution in the U.S. context, I did not include data from persons who had recently arrived from Puerto Rico.

Although the stories collected are on a range of subjects, they are all oral narratives of past events. This means that I can compare the performance of the same discourse unit, a narrative of past experience, extracted from interviews about Latino life on Long Island, despite other differences in the stories told.

This study provides an integrative approach to language study. I bring together a description of the sociolinguistic patterns of the community gathered through participant observation (chap. 1) with a more general analysis of language use and attitude patterns gleaned from a survey distributed to more than 300 community members (chap. 2). The results of these analyses point to the fact that although young Puerto Ricans in Brentwood still use Spanish in the home, they use Spanish exclusively less frequently than older community members. With this important base established, in chapter 3, I analyze linguistic features of the Spanish language narratives produced by Spanish-dominant, bilingual, and English-dominant Puerto Ricans. Despite differences in language proficiency, I find that from the perspective of narrative structure and grammar, particularly the use of verb patterns and syntactic complexity, all three groups are more similar than different. In chapter 4, I explore the significant differences between the English-dominant speakers and the others in terms of the integration of English into Spanish-discourse at the lexical level. I also demonstrate how English-dominant speakers are more apt than the other two groups to use creative and innovate techniques such as code-switching and certain types of borrowing. In chapter 5, I take a closer look at the content of the narratives. Specifically, I analyze how internalized racism and sexism is both reproduced and resisted in the narratives of Brentwood Puerto Ricans. Although internalized oppression is apparent in the discourse of community members, there is also ample evidence that they resist such negative sentiments. Analysis of the narratives shows that community members, particularly the younger English-dominant speakers, often use an explicit and direct language to name and confront sexism and racism.

In the conclusion, I summarize how the study of macro- (societal factors) and micro- (linguistic forms and constructions) sociolinguistic features of the Brentwood Puerto Ricans yields an integrative perspective on Spanish language use in the community. I also discuss the implications of my study. My research makes clear that future study of Spanish in the United States would be enhanced by a focus on individual communities and their own unique set of societal dynamics. At the same time, given the linguistic and social diversity that exists in each community, a multifaceted approach to sociolinguistic research is undoubtedly warranted.

1

The Brentwood
Puerto Rican Community

INTRODUCTION

For a 3-year period, from 1989 to 1991, I engaged in ethnographic research in Brentwood, participating in and observing public and private interactions in the Puerto Rican community. As a Puerto Rican woman who had lived in Brentwood, Long Island for a number of years as a teenager, I easily gained access to the community. I participated in Latino-focused social, cultural, and political events in the town. These activities afforded me formal and informal contact with the participants in the study and their family and friends. I engaged in the planning of educational, cultural, and political programs and also attended parties and other social affairs. Thus, I was able to observe community linguistic behavior in a variety of situations, ranging from informal family gatherings in homes to formal public meetings and political activities.

Whereas chapter 2 reviews the findings of an anonymous questionnaire on language use and attitudes distributed to over 300 community members, in this chapter I present my insights on the role of the Spanish language in the life of the community based on the ethnographic research in Brentwood with Puerto Ricans; also included are observations made by participants during our conversations. The combination of macro- and micromethodologies in these two chapters yields a complex and multifaceted perspective on language use in the community.

PUERTO RICANS AND OTHER LATINOS
IN LONG ISLAND, NY

The migration of Puerto Ricans to the United States dates back to the mid-1800s and increased substantially when the United States invaded Puerto Rico in 1898. Since then there have been certain periods of intense migration, especially in the 1950s after World War II. Although the migration of Puerto Ricans to the New York City area, where most Puerto Ricans originally settled, has been studied extensively, and some attention has been directed to such other urban Puerto Rican communities as Philadelphia and Chicago, little is known of the Puerto Rican enclaves in other areas. According to the 1992 census, approximately 43% of all Latinos live in suburbia, and this number is dramatically increasing. This statistic alone underscores the importance of focusing on Latino populations in nonmetropolitan areas (Frey, 1993).

Suffolk County, Long Island has the largest Latino community in New York State outside New York City. According to census estimates, in suburban Long Island, from 1980 to 1990, the Hispanic population increased by 62%, growing from 101,975 to 165,238 persons. From 1980 to 1990 Suffolk County's Latino population grew 50% from 58,689 to 87,852. Community leaders claim that the increase is much larger than these figures suggest, because Latinos tend to be undercounted in the census.

The town of Brentwood, site of this study, has the largest Latino population in Suffolk County. According to the 1980 census, 22% of Brentwood's residents were of Hispanic origin, and 78% of that group self-identified as Puerto Rican. By 1990, 15,692 out of 45,218 persons—or 35%—of people in this community, self-identified as Hispanic. Puerto Ricans first settled in Brentwood during the 1930s, encouraged by the promise of inexpensive land, housing, and jobs in agriculture; at $150.00 an acre, many became land owners. Unlike other places where Latino immigration followed other migrants, Puerto Ricans were part of the original settling population in the 22-square mile radius known as Brentwood (Guanil, 1980). In the 1950s, a sizable influx of Puerto Ricans arrived in Brentwood to take jobs in the expanding industries (especially at Pilgrim State Hospital, an expansive state-run mental hospital, and Entenmann's Bakery, a large-scale plant). A lower-middle class and working-class community has continued to grow since then (Long Island Regional Planning Board, 1981). The 1970s again brought a large migration of Puerto Ricans to Brentwood, primarily from the New York City area. According to the 1980 census, approximately one fourth of the Hispanic families in Brentwood can be identified as middle class, whereas 75% are working class or fall below the federally defined poverty line. Whereas new Latino immigrants have changed the dynamics of the community in ways that I develop in forthcoming sections, Puerto Ricans continue to be the largest Latino subgroup in Brentwood.

Of all the immigrants that have made Brentwood their home, Latinos are the only group to establish a thriving ethnic enclave. Puerto Ricans dominate the Latino community in terms of numbers, history in the community, and presence in Latino organizations. Many social, political, and cultural organizations cater to Latino interests and needs, and the Latino community makes its presence felt via a number of highly visible activities. Every Sunday, hundreds of Latinos congregate in local fields to watch as players in a Latin American soccer league compete. Latino vendors work the area selling everything from food to Latino music tapes. Throughout the year local organizations, such as Adelante and the Brentwood Recreation Center, sponsor workshops for children and young adults in Latino dancing and other cultural activities. The second Sunday in June is Latin American Day in Brentwood; a Puerto Rican parade highlights this annual celebration.

The greatest concentration of Hispanics in Brentwood is located in an area known as *El Barrio*, named after the well-known Puerto Rican neighborhood in New York City. The main avenue that runs through this area is lined with Latino-owned restaurants, grocery stores, botánicas, barber shops, other businesses, and social clubs. When walking through the area one can always hear Latino music playing from many stores and Spanish spoken everywhere.

Since the 1980s, a large number of Latinos have arrived in Long Island from Central and South America, especially El Salvador, Guatemala, and Colombia; Dominicans from the Caribbean have also added to the rapidly increasing population. This new, often undocumented influx has brought approximately 50,000 to 100,000 persons to Long Island. Many have settled in Brentwood, adding an entirely new dimension to the Latino community.

A mostly poor and uneducated population, the latest Latino immigrants face tremendous obstacles in securing everything from medical care, to education, and to decent housing. Drawn to Long Island during the 1980s when the economy was booming, they responded to the need for unskilled labor. The restaurant business, as well as light industries and factories, have benefitted greatly from the arrival of a large labor force, composed of persons who, because of their dire circumstances, are cheaper to hire than other Long Islanders. Given their status as undocumented workers, they are often reluctant to participate in Puerto Rican-initiated and Puerto Rican-dominated civic and social organizations. Relations between the more established Puerto Rican community and the new Latino immigrants are sometimes strained. Although the social services set up to aid the Puerto Rican community have focused some of their efforts on the special needs of the new undocumented immigrants, mixed feelings abound about their presence in the community. Some Puerto Rican long-time factory workers who have been laid off feel that because business owners can pay undocumented workers less, and because these workers do not participate in union activities or attempts to unionize shops, they are preferred by employers.

Additionally, the housing situation of the recent immigrants draws the ire of some Puerto Ricans who have saved and slaved all their lives for a house in the suburbs. Now they witness absentee landlords in their neighborhoods renting houses or apartments to the newcomers, who sometimes must pool their resources and live together in large numbers in order to afford exorbitant rents. Many Brentwood residents are torn by a desire to help the immigrants and a concern about how their presence affects the property values of the community. One long-time home owner expresses sympathy for the newcomers at the same time that she voices concern for her neighborhood:

> *Había una (casa) de como quince (personas) en una casa, le quitaron la luz, le quitaron el agua, y tú veías, ellos yendo hasta donde está las pompas de agua con ollas en la cabeza, ir a buscar agua, y cosas así afectan la comunidad hispana, especialmente si la comunidad hispana está tratando de superarse, y en Brentwood hay muchos hispanos que adoran a Brentwood, que nunca piensan irse de ahí y se sienten ofendidos de que nunca van a poder prosperar como un pueblo hispano.*

> [There was a house with about fifteen people in the house, they turned off the electricity, they turned off the water, and you could see them going up to where the water hydrants are with pots of water on their heads, go to get water, and things like that affect the Hispanic community, especially if the Hispanic community is trying to better itself, and in Brentwood there are many Hispanics who love Brentwood, who never think about leaving and they feel offended because they will never be able to prosper as a Latino community.]

It remains to be seen whether the older and newer communities will eventually merge or grow apart. Although the population dynamics continue to change, most of the Latino organizations in Brentwood are still, as of 1995, predominantly run by Puerto Ricans, who also make up the vast majority of the membership. Some of the leaders of these groups believe that as jobs become scarce, new immigrants will leave Brentwood for New York City or other urban areas where they can find employment; but for now the most recent community members seem determined to make a life for themselves as best they can in Brentwood.

LANGUAGE USE IN PUBLIC DOMAINS

Spanish is generally heard in the businesses and shops that line Fifth Avenue, the heart of the Latino commercial district in Brentwood. In the bodegas, restaurants, liquor stores, and jewelry stores, most of the employees and customers are Latinos, and Spanish, for the most part, is the language of commerce. Adults are always addressed in Spanish, although teenagers and children are spoken to in English by those employees who speak English. When I asked why they address young people in English, several employees indicated that often the young people are reluctant to converse in Spanish. One grocer remarked, *"ellos entienden, yo sé que entienden, pero no lo quieren hablar y por eso yo les hablo en inglés."* ["They understand it, I know that they understand but they don't want to speak it and that's why I speak to them in English."]

Latino men often congregate in front of the small shopping centers where conversations are frequently in Spanish with some code-mixing. The Latino adults are from many backgrounds: Puerto Ricans, Dominicans, and Central Americans. Women also converse outdoors, but usually in front of homes and often in the company of children. The older women tend to communicate in Spanish and code-mixing, whereas younger women speak English, or code-mix, and less often speak Spanish. Some of the young adults do not speak Spanish unless they are interacting with Spanish monolinguals.

Social service organizations, such as La Unión Hispánica, are other public places where Spanish is frequently heard. La Unión Hispánica is a large referral agency that services the community by helping Latinos find employment, affordable housing, legal aid, immigration assistance, English classes, prenatal care, and other services. The majority of the employees at La Unión are Puerto Rican, and all are bilingual; most are English-dominant, and a small percentage is Spanish-dominant. The clients, on the other hand, are primarily Spanish monolingual or Spanish-dominant; among themselves and in their interactions with employees they speak Spanish. Young Puerto Ricans who are employed at social service agencies such as La Unión explained to me that because of their work they experience a reactivation of Spanish language skills that they may have allowed to become passive. One 25-year-old woman commented:

> *Estoy mejorando mi español desde que empecé a trabajar aquí, es una de las cosas que más me gusta de este trabajo. Personalmente, me gustaría hablar el español perfectamente.*
>
> [I am improving my Spanish since I began to work here, it is one of the things that I like best about this job. Personally, I would like to speak Spanish perfectly.]

Churches are another site where Spanish is often heard, particularly in the evangelical churches. A 1980 survey reported that 75% of all Latinos are affiliated with a church and 35% of these regularly attend services in Spanish (Rosenberg, 1981). In fact, church functions are the community activities most frequented by Latinos in Brentwood. Spanish-speaking churches are vibrant, busy places in the community. Although most of the participants in the churches are monolingual, first generation adults, the Spanish-speaking churches do make an effort to incorporate youngsters in their activities; they conduct many of these functions geared toward children in Spanish. A few of the churches even have Spanish language classes for children and young adults. Thus, the church serves as an important site for Spanish language maintenance.

This is not the case for the Catholic churches in Brentwood, which conduct masses exclusively in English. Although a few of the more progressive Catholic churches do provide some religious services in Spanish, it is the evangelical churches that specifically serve the Spanish-speaking population. Many of these are led by Latino (primarily Puerto Rican) ministers, who make an effort to reach out to Latinos by providing a wide range of programs in their language. In addition to holding religious services in Spanish, some provide child care, counselling services, immigration help, English classes, food distribution, and other services.

Compared to other public spaces, it was at activities sponsored by the evangelical churches where I most frequently heard interactions in Spanish, even among the children and young people. Although female church participants predominate, male participants are also centrally involved in church related activities. One 24-year-old Puerto Rican man explained to me that it was through his involvement with the church that he began to use Spanish again, after distancing himself from the language in his adolescence. He claimed that he was not unique; many of his friends also spoke Spanish more often once they became integrated in the church. This enthusiastic young man stated that his Spanish-speaking church was so attractive that even English speakers attended services there; bilingual Puerto Rican young people sit by them and translate for them, or else Anglos attend weekly programs where the church teachings are explained in English. When I asked him why English monolingual Americans would attend his church, he replied:

> *Bueno es bien claro porque, you know, yo estaba hablando con una muchacha que vino y se quiere quedar en el program de español, entonces yo le dije por qué, por qué tú no vas a una iglesia en inglés—no, no la tratan con el cariño que los puertorriqueño le tratan, so entonces hay un acercamiento entre loh latinos que no se encuentra en ningún otro sitio.*

> [Well it is very clear why, you know, I was speaking with a girl who came and she wants to stay in the Spanish program, then I said why, why don't you go to an English church—they don't treat her with the kindness that the Puerto Ricans treat her with, so then there is a closeness among Latinos that one can't find in any other place.]

The church is thus a strong force in the Brentwood community and one of the institutions that actively supports the use and maintenance of Spanish. Many church leaders express the opinion that children and young people should learn about Latino culture and traditions and they feel the Spanish language is an important element in this endeavor.

In contrast, in the social and cultural public meetings of all the Latino organizations I observed, most business is conducted in English. In the meetings I attended and observed, an average of 90% of all the participants were Puerto Rican; interestingly, Spanish and code-mixing were heard only occasionally, in private conversations between individual members. Sometimes a *"Buenas noches"* initiates the meetings but then English predominates. Even Puerto Ricans who are obviously Spanish-dominant speak exclusively in English when addressing the entire group. These persons tend to speak Spanish among themselves, but always accommodate English speakers who join their conversation. I asked a Spanish-dominant woman at a political event why all the speakers who were Puerto Rican were addressing the entirely Puerto Rican audience in English. She responded, *"Es que aunque la mayoría de la gente habla español, hay algunos que no lo entienden bien, y por cortesía se tiende a hablar en inglés. Pero creo que también deberíamos hablar más en español"* ["It is that although the majority of the people speak Spanish, there are a few that don't understand it well and we tend to speak English out of courtesy. But I think also that we should speak Spanish more."] It seems clear that English is the implicitly agreed on language of official business in formal public places.

LATINO/LATINA LANGUAGE-RELATED COMMUNITY ACTIVISM

Brentwood is home to many Latino/Latina political organizations such as Long Island Hispanic Forum, a chapter of the National Congress of Puerto Rican Women, Hispanic Outreach Committee, and organizations designed to provide services to the Latino community, such as La Unión Hispánica, Los Latinos de Long Island, and Adelante. For many years, Latino organizers have run Hispanic candidates in local elections. When the traditional Democratic and Republican parties have refused to sponsor particular Latino candidates, talk of initiating a Latino Political Party has emerged. However, few Hispanics have won political office on Long Island. A Puerto Rican woman who ran an unsuccessful campaign for Town Supervisor was later appointed head of the Human Rights Commission. Other Latino politicians continue to make a difference for the Latino community through their involvement in Long Island politics at the grassroots level.

In recent years, Brentwood has faced two important situations that have focused attention on language rights. The controversies surrounding bilingual education and the introduction of an English Only Bill served to inspire Puerto Rican political activity at many levels. The Latino community was divided in its analysis of these questions. Although many Puerto Ricans support bilingual education and were against English-only laws, some favored the status quo positions on these issues. Here, and in chapter 5, I analyze such responses suggesting that those who are against bilingual education and favor English-only bills have accepted the dominant group ideology and are articulating what can be considered "internalized oppression."

The quest for meaningful education for children with limited English proficiency continues to concern community leaders. Brentwood, a school district with a 35% Latino population, has experimented with various bilingual and immersion programs. Although many of the Puerto Ricans I spoke with support bilingual education, others do not. One woman, a second-generation Puerto Rican who learned English via the "sink or swim" method in the 1950s, explains why she opposes bilingual education:

> I always felt that bilingual education was good but not the way they are administering it because now the kid stands out like a sore thumb and whether people like it or not it affects them, it traumatizes them, he's different then, he begins to feel that he is different and then he behaves differently which is the worst part. I always felt that bilingual education should—the child should go to school and have his classes in English, with difficulty but kids are like rubber they bounce around, at the end of the day if they wanted to be bilingual then they should say this is what you learned today in Spanish. And he wouldn't have to go to a special class, now he wasn't pointed out.

Interestingly, another woman from the same generation, who came to New York as a child, strongly disagrees with this position. Speaking about people who oppose bilingual education, she states:

> *Quizás esa personas nunca tuvieron la experiencia que yo tuve. Si ellos hubieran tenido la experiencia que yo estuve [tuve] entonces ellos dirían no, el programa bilingüe es una gran cosa. Yo no estuve [tuve] esa ayuda, si yo la hubiera tenido, yo no hubiera tenido que dejar la escuela, porque a mí me gustaba la escuela pero la frustración de que como no entendía, y yo trataba, trataba lo más posible, y entonces me salí, no quise más, no quise más, no quise, no quise, porque era una frustración tremenda.*

> [Maybe those persons never had the experience that I had. If they would have had the experience that I had they would say no, the bilingual program is a great thing. I didn't have that help, if I would have had it, I would not have had to leave school, because I liked school but the frustration because I didn't understand, and I tried, I tried as much as possible, and then I left, I couldn't any more, I couldn't anymore, I couldn't, I couldn't, because it was a tremendous frustration.]

Since the 1960s when Puerto Ricans came to Brentwood in large numbers, parents and school administrators have been wrangling over ways to provide the most effective education for Hispanic children. In the early 1970s the district had an award-winning bilingual education program in the elementary schools, which sought to maintain and enhance the children's Spanish language skills at the same time as it developed their ability to function academically in English. In June 1978, during a budget crisis, the district announced that it was dismissing 18 of the 24 bilingual education teachers and, for all intents and purposes, eliminating the program. A group of Latino parents organized and sued the district. The presiding judge, District Judge Jacob Misher, ruled that the bilingual program was unacceptable and in violation of federal laws and guidelines because Latino children were in self-contained classrooms and therefore isolated from the mainstream population in the schools. However, Judge Misher also ruled as unacceptable the district's plan to simply mainstream the children. The program then underwent many modifications in the late 1970s and early 1980s.

During the years of my work in the community (1989–1991) what remained was a structure that few would recognize as bilingual education. Since the late 1980s, the programs for children of limited proficiency in English vary according to academic level. A pull-out bilingual program is available in some of the elementary schools. Children who test at a very low level of proficiency in English are pulled from their regular classes and given two hours of bilingual classes a day. Children who score somewhat higher receive two hours of ESL a day. In the junior high schools, ESL is the preferred method, with one out of four schools serving all the kids at the junior high level needing linguistic services. The high school is divided into a 10th grade center, and an 11th and 12th grade center. In the 10th grade center, students can receive up to two periods of ESL. There is no ESL past this stage; in the 11th and 12th grade centers, students are mainstreamed with the rest of the school population. At every level the objective is to mainstream the children into English language classes as soon as possible.

With the great influx of Central Americans in the 1980s, the Brentwood schools' monolingual Spanish population increased significantly. This growth has created problems which continue to challenge the district. For example, Spanish monolingual, illiterate children, arriving from Central American countries, who are placed in the junior high schools, are expected to be mainstreamed into the high school after 3 years, regardless of whether they can function in English. The children experience intense frustration and this likely contributes to the high drop out rate in the high schools. Officially, the overall dropout rate for all high school students is 4% (Wolfson, 1991), whereas for Latino students it is 15% (Somos Uno Conference Report, 1989); however, there is a community-wide suspicion that the rate is much higher, especially at the high school level, given the fact that after the 10th grade, all limited English proficiency students are mainstreamed regardless of their academic and linguistic preparation.

Many teachers and counselors who work with Spanish-dominant children express dissatisfaction with the system and with the inadequate number of bilingual professionals hired by the district. Brentwood has few bilingual education and ESL teachers, and even fewer teachers of Hispanic descent. A 1989 conference report indicates that only 4% of the staff is of Latino background (Somos Uno Conference Report, 1989).

Many challenges face students with limited English proficiency; thus far, education administrators in Brentwood have not successfully addressed the issues that emerge in a community that each year becomes increasingly more multicultural and multilingual. One former teacher in Brentwood states:

> It was the administration and the district officials who decided not to put in a decent bilingual program. In the long run the Hispanic community comes out short, on the short end of the stick. They dismantled the bilingual program and we ended up in Brentwood, in my opinion, losing. They should know that Hispanics are the largest growing population. By the year 2020 some statisticians are saying that one out of every four births is going to be a Hispanic child. The schools haven't been doing long range planning; they aren't going to be prepared for this.

Given the illegal status and unstable situation of many Central and South Americans who move to Brentwood, Latino parental involvement in the school organizations has fallen in the last decade. However, many parents and community leaders continue to fight for the educational rights of the children.

That the ethnic composition of Brentwood is changing has not been lost on the residents in the area. Such rapid transformation can be frightening to other long-established ethnic groups who fear that their way of life is threatened. During the time I worked in the Brentwood community, the local government considered declaring English the official language of Suffolk County. This is a part of the xenophobic response to the rise in immigration from Latin America and Asia in the last decades that has spawned a nationwide English-only movement. In 1989, a Republican legislator in Suffolk County sponsored a bill that would have placed this issue on the ballot as a binding referendum. He stated that he was motivated to introduce the English Only Bill when the County Executive suggested that there was a need to hire bilingual workers at state offices to provide services to Spanish monolingual people. The English Only Bill, which was eventually defeated as a result of the active and persistent efforts of Puerto Rican community leaders and citizens, would have mandated that all official county business be conducted in English. The bill would have ended the practice of printing informational brochures in Spanish and would have prohibited all county employees from speaking Spanish in the workplace. Exempted from the measure were voting and registration materials and such public safety concerns as 911 operators.

The public hearings held to debate the question were well attended by proponents and opponents of the bill. Many proponents stressed their desire for harmony and unity under one language, whereas others attacked Hispanics for not learning English. At one public hearing, a veteran proclaimed, "We didn't go to war to bring the foreign people over here. We left them over there" (Gray, 1989). Latinos, both Puerto Ricans and other national groups, were the most numerous opponents of the bill at the meetings, but many Anglos also spoke out against it.

Most Puerto Ricans I spoke with agreed that English was the de facto official language of the country, and that everyone who desired to live in the United States should learn English; however, most Puerto Ricans spoke out against enacting such a law. Many felt that the bill was aimed at restricting the rights of the Latino community. One second generation adult male expresses his opinion this way:

> *A veces en mi trabajo hay empleados que su lenguaje dominante es español. Yo a veces estoy con ellos. Estamos en coffee break y están hablando español y no, y hay este,* "Hey speak English you, you're in America." *Y yo siempre le digo* and because we're in America we have the freedom to know any language and speak any language we want.

> [Sometimes at my job there are employees whose dominant language is Spanish. I am sometimes with them. We are on coffee break and they are speaking Spanish and no, and then, "Hey speak English, you're in America." And I always say to them and because we are in America we have the freedom to know any language and speak any language we want.]

Others indicated that although most Puerto Ricans are bilingual, they fight against the English-only law because it is discriminatory against newcomers. Another second-generation Puerto Rican male explains:

> Okay, *nosotros, yo no estoy luchando por mí, porque dondequiera que me meta voy a salir bien, pero yo estoy luchando para la gente que están entrando a este país, que ellos están discriminando contra esa gente, porque según vinieron los abuelos míos aquí,* right, *y ellos entraron por ese problema so nosotros estamos peleando por esa gente, no por los hijos míos, no por los nietos míos, sino por los que están entrando ahora.*

> [Okay we, I am not fighting for me, because wherever I go I will come out alright, but I am fighting for the people who are coming into this country, because they are discriminating against those people, because just like my grandparents came here, right, and they came into that problem so we are fighting for those people, not for my children, not for my grandchildren, rather for the ones that are coming now.]

On the other hand, a small number of Puerto Ricans supported the English Only Bill. Those who held this position tended to believe the dominant group argument that such legislation would serve as an incentive for Latinos to learn English. One woman explains:

Según los surveys *que se han hecho en* Long Island *el setenta por ciento de la gente piensan que es buena idea. Si tenemos al* English Only *puede ser para ayudar al latino, o cualquier raza que entra, para ellos poder aprender el idioma para poder defenderse en el trabajo o en la vida. Claro, estoy de acuerdo con eso.*

[According to the surveys that have been done on Long Island, 70% of the people think it's a good idea. If we have English Only it could be to help the Latino or any other race that arrives so that they could learn the language so they could defend themselves at work and in life. Of course I am in favor of that.]

Although the English Only bill was resoundingly defeated in Brentwood, its introduction and consideration indicate a certain level of fear and resentment on the part of non-Latino residents, due to the undeniably changing face of the community. In chapter 5, I explore the phenomenon of those Puerto Ricans who support English-only laws and other status quo arguments.

Language issues also arose in other areas during the years I participated in the community. Because of complaints that the police were rude and dismissive towards Spanish monolingual speakers, in 1991, the Suffolk County Human Rights Commission began to secretly record phone calls to the police precinct in Brentwood. For example, a call from a resident in distress was recorded in which the attending police officer told the caller, "If you can't speak English, tough luck" (Olojede, 1991). This situation prompted an outcry from the Latino community and forced the police department to take steps to make officers more responsive to the many Latino residents in their district. Of the 222 police in the Brentwood precinct, only 22 were Latinos and only 12 others could speak any Spanish. The precinct hired a Spanish-speaking operator and a Spanish language course was offered, which was taken by 19 officers. Additionally, officers attended workshops aimed at familiarizing them with Latino cultural practices. A local women's coalition, which runs a battered women's shelter, also convinced the department that a Spanish-speaking member from the coalition should accompany officers when they respond to domestic violence complaints in Brentwood. As of the time I completed my fieldwork in Brentwood, the police department was slowly acknowledging the fact that it had a responsibility to sensitize the largely White police officers to the cultural and linguistic realities of the community.

Despite the fact that many people I spoke with described instances of ethnic, racial, or language discrimination directed at them or family and friends, others declared that they had never experienced any type of discrimination at all. One 55-year-old, first-generation woman responded as follows when I asked her if she had ever been discriminated on the basis of language:

> *Yo nunca podría decir, sinceramente, yo vine hace quince años atrás y como he sido una persona bien positiva, tú da lo que tú tienes, y según lo que tú tienes así te tratan.*

> [I could never say, sincerely, I came here 15 years ago and because I have been a really positive person, you give what you have, and according to what you have that's how you are treated.]

Other residents feel that, whereas the new immigrants experience outright discrimination, the discrimination faced by the more established Puerto Ricans is more subtle and difficult to prove. For example, during their interview with me several people mentioned that Puerto Rican employees face a glass ceiling in the workplace. One woman states:

> *Los puertorriqueños sufren discriminación en términos del trabajo. Uno ve que una persona que trabaja en un lugar varios años y cada vez la pasan para puestos más importantes, y no pueden decir, uno no puede probar actualmente, fue porque soy puertorriqueña, pero por eso mismo fue.*

> [Puerto Ricans suffer discrimination in terms of work. One sees that a person that works at a place several years and they always pass her by for important promotions, and they can't say, one can't actually prove it, it was because I'm Puerto Rican, but that's exactly why it was.]

Still others in the community blame Puerto Ricans themselves for any problems that they might experience. Some Puerto Ricans have internalized racist ideology concerning their own people. One woman explains why Anglos discriminate against Puerto Ricans in the following manner:

> *Sí hay discriminación, pero a veces es nuestra culpa. El puertorriqueño no quiere trabajar. Lo que quiere es estar viviendo del Welfare y tener todo. Ellos quieren—no tienen high school y quieren ganar nueve pesos la hora. No son orgullosos.*

> [Yes there is discrimination, but sometimes it is our fault. Puerto Ricans don't want to work. What they want is to be living off Welfare and have everything, They want—they don't have high school and they want to earn nine dollars an hour. They aren't proud.]

Although such opinions do not represent the general perspective of the Puerto Rican community, they did occur in some interviews. I explore such viewpoints as manifestations of internalized oppression in chapter 5.

LANGUAGE USE IN PRIVATE DOMAINS

During the 3 years of my work in the community, I also observed informal language use during visits to the homes of Brentwood residents with whom I became acquainted. Often, these were social occasions where family and friends were present.

Class differences in language use exist, with more Spanish spoken in the working-class homes and English favored in the middle-class homes. Here I define class loosely on the basis of education and occupation. Working-class persons are those who have less than a high school education and are employed as blue collar workers, for example, as factory workers, sewing machine operators, or service employees. The middle-class are persons with more than a high school education, employed as white collar workers or professionals in the community. This category includes teachers, health professionals, social workers, and so on.

First-generation people and those who are recent arrivals to the United States speak Spanish in the home regardless of class. Many of the adults I observed, who were between 50 and 65 years old, were second-generation, meaning that either they were born in the United States or had immigrated at a very early age. Those second-generation adults who were educated, studied for the most part at English monolingual schools, but continued to speak Spanish at home when they were growing up. In the working-class homes, among this age group, Spanish is used exclusively, or frequently predominates. In middle-class homes, however, English predominates among second-generation adults of this age group.

Because the two groups have similar backgrounds, in terms of age and time in the United States, the difference in language preference is explained by class itself, that is education and employment histories. Many of the working-class persons have less than a high school education and are employed primarily as factory workers or machine operators in environments where most of their coworkers are Spanish-speaking. The middle-class group typically has had a more formal education in English and many of its members have attended college. Additionally, they are primarily involved in work situations where English predominates or is used exclusively. Most of the middle-class persons have social networks that include non-Spanish-speaking Anglos, while this is not generally the case for the working-class Latinos.

The adult children of both the middle-class and working-class participants, those between the ages of 18 and 30, were born and raised on Long Island. They are all bilingual and most are English-dominant. Some are passive bilinguals, meaning that they understand Spanish but can not speak it with ease. Although all the young people I interviewed were able to converse with me in Spanish, some felt insecure about their abilities. One young woman comments about her language: *"Mi español está un poquito estruja'o."* ["My Spanish is a bit wrinkled."] Another comments: *"Mi español es terrible.* I'm serious." ["My Spanish is terrible."] Although all persons in this group understand Spanish, few use Spanish unless they are speaking with Spanish monolingual family members or friends. If addressed in Spanish by parents or grandparents who understand English, many reply in English or code-mix.

In the households I visited, many young children speak English primarily. However, in those homes where older monolingual persons such as grandparents and other relatives reside, the children are addressed in Spanish and it is clear that they understand Spanish even if they reply in English or code-mix. The language of the caretakers determines the language of the very young children, but once the child leaves the home to attend school this pattern changes. All of the parents express a desire for their children to be bilingual, but the actual effort exerted to realize this goal is often not sufficient. A 37-year-old, second-generation mother of two explains:

Yo le dije a mi esposo que mis niños van a hablar español. So decidimos que íbamos a usar un idioma primero y después íbamos a cambiar a inglés. Lo que sucedió fue que hasta los tres años mi niño fue siempre criado por una mexicana, una colombiana, so aprendió un español bello, muy bonito. A los tres años empezó a ir a la escuela conmigo, en la escuela no habían hispanos, la única era yo. So él empezó a captar el inglés. So decidimos cambiar en casa, yo hablaba inglés y mi esposo hablaba español, pero mi esposo no siguió el español so en los años el niño no se hizo bilingüe sino monolingüe. Entiende español pero no lo habla, pero lo está hablando ahora porque lo está estudiando.

[I told my husband that my children are going to speak Spanish. So we decided that we were going to speak one language first and then we were going to change to English. What happened was that until he was three my son was always cared for by a Mexican, a Colombian, so he learned a beautiful Spanish, very nice. At the age of three he began to come to school with me, in school there were no Hispanics, I was the only one. So he began to pick up English. So we decided to change at home, I spoke English and my husband spoke Spanish, but my husband didn't keep up with the Spanish so as time passed my son didn't become bilingual but monolingual. He understands Spanish but doesn't speak it, but now he is speaking it because he is studying it.]

Many parents speak of their efforts to raise bilingual children, but even when there are primarily monolingual persons in the household, once children begin school, most often English becomes the dominant language. Spanish assumes a more passive status until the time that the child decides to make an effort to use Spanish. Sometimes, the language skills of the children raised in the same context are different; a Spanish-dominant first generation woman makes the following observations about her teenage children:

> *Yo siempre le he hablado en español a mis hijos. La niña habla el español bastante bien, lo lee y lo escribe un poco y el varón no me habla nada de español. Pero quizá sea porque la nena siempre estaba conmigo, siempre estaba en casa, y el varón estaba más afuera.*

> [I have always spoken Spanish to my children. The girl speaks Spanish rather well, she reads it and writes it a bit and the boy doesn't speak any Spanish. But maybe it is because the girl was always with me, she was always at home, and the boy was outside more often.]

Many factors interact in determining the language choices of children. The dominant language of the primary caretakers is obviously central, especially early on, but then age, sex, peer group associations, employment, school, and church involvement are all factors that influence language choice as well. As we have seen, adolescents and young adults who become integrated in Spanish-speaking adult networks in the church or at work may experience a revitalization of their Spanish language skills. Young Puerto Ricans, dominant in English, who marry Spanish-dominant or monolingual people, may also feel the need to engage in a Spanish-speaking world again. As one teenage woman points out:

> *Yo cuando lo conocí a él casi no hablaba espanol, lo entendía y to' pero casi no lo hablaba nunca, pero como él no sabía nada de inglés, empecé a hablar más español,* and now we speak Spanish most of the time.

> [When I met him I hardly ever spoke Spanish, I understood it and all but I hardly ever spoke it, but because he didn't know any English, I began to speak more Spanish, and now we speak Spanish most of the time.]

Language choice and use is clearly a dynamic matter that continues to evolve across the lifespan of each individual.

In summary, this short description provides a brief glimpse at the role of Spanish in the public and private life of the Brentwood Puerto Rican community as I was able to observe it. In chapter 2, I analyze the results of a language behavior survey in order to provide an overview of reported Spanish and English language use.

Language Maintenance and Shift in Brentwood

INTRODUCTION

In this chapter, following a review of pertinent research involving language use surveys, I describe the function and status of Spanish and English in the Brentwood Puerto Rican bilingual community through a discussion of the findings of a language use and attitudes survey that I administered. Whereas in the previous chapter I described the use of Spanish as observed in private and public domains, here I consider the results of a survey that captures community assessment of language use.

The results of the survey suggest that, across generations, Spanish is used less than English. At the same time, in most cases Puerto Ricans report using both languages rather than either Spanish or English exclusively. Thus, whereas speakers have retained few Spanish-only domains, there are also few English-only domains in Brentwood households; rather, both languages more or less coexist across domains. Although code-switching is a common phenomenon for both parents and children, the majority of speakers I studied are ambivalent as to its use. Speakers seem to have internalized prescriptions against the use of two languages in a single utterance, but at the same time they continue to engage in such linguistic behavior. Although Puerto Ricans of all ages report that both languages are important to them, English is valued for instrumental reasons while Spanish is important for affective reasons. In terms of gender differences across generations in language use, whereas a higher percentage of adult males report speaking Spanish exclusively, it is female students who report speaking more Spanish. These differences are best explained by referring to the ethnographic data.

Overall, although a superficial reading of the survey data may suggest that Spanish is being lost in the community, close analysis of the sociolinguistic dynamics at play in Brentwood, as well as the ethnographic data reported in chapter 1, forestalls this conclusion. The sociolinguistic dynamics of relevance include the constant influx of

Spanish-speakers in Brentwood and the involvement of young people in community activities where Spanish predominantes. Also, the study of the structure of Spanish-speaking narratives in chapters 3 and 4 leads to a more positive assessment of the future of Spanish in Brentwood.

Determining the language maintenance or shift patterns of a community is a complex process that entails consideration of many variables. As Giles, Bourhis, and Taylor (1979) suggest, the vitality or maintenance of a minority language must be assessed in terms of both micro and macro factors that influence language use. At the micro level, the internal dynamics of community language use, such as when, where, and how often the minority language is spoken, and the community's attitude about language varieties are relevant. Important macro or external factors that should also be analyzed include: migration patterns, media support (newspapers, television and radio programs in the minority language), outgroup community attitudes, and institutional support such as bilingual programs.

LANGUAGE USE AND ATTITUDES STUDIES

Many studies have investigated Spanish language retention and loss in the United States (Fishman, Cooper, & Ma, 1971; García et al., 1988; Hart-González & Feingold, 1990; LPTF, 1982; Pedraza, 1985; Solé, 1990; Veltman, 1983; Zentella, 1985). Whereas a few studies (e.g., Pedraza, 1985) argue that the Hispanic case offers a divergence from the typical immigrant pattern of language loss across three generations, most (e.g., Veltman, 1983) suggest that Hispanics follow the same pattern but may retain Spanish somewhat longer than other ethnic groups. As with all groups, as the length of residence increases, so does usage of the English language. Veltman (1983) reports that all second generation ethnic groups except Hispanics shift to English monolingualism. Second-generation Hispanics are English-dominant, but they retain Spanish so that various levels of bilingualism are present for this group as opposed to other ethnic communities. This bilingualism, however, is said to be transitional because 50% of the children of this second generation are English monolingual by the time they are 18 years old.

Hart-González and Feingold (1990) examine 1979 census data to study language maintenance, shift, and loss in U.S. Hispanic communities. They observe a clear tendency toward home language shift in all Hispanic communities. Hart-González and Feingold examine the size and relationship between subgroups of Hispanics as this is related to maintenance. They find that for most groups (except Cubans and South Americans), "in a large ethnic subgroup, a larger pan-Hispanic community is associated with greater loss of Spanish" (Hart-González, 1990, p. 29). Whereas some researchers such as Pedraza (1985) speculate that the large influx of Latinos means greater visibility and mass media support for the Spanish language in communities like New York, Hart-González (1985) believes that in the pan-Hispanic community of Washington, Spanish language use in the subgroup rather than the existence of a pan-Hispanic community, is most important for maintenance.

As more and more Hispanics from countries other than Mexico, Puerto Rico, and Cuba come to Brentwood and establish themselves in what was previously a Puerto Rican enclave, one has to consider the effect of this pan-Hispanic phenomenon on Spanish language maintenance. Although it can not be assumed that the mere influx of more Spanish speakers will encourage Spanish language maintenance in Brentwood, it is true that their presence has brought more institutional support in the form of an increase in Spanish-speaking churches and media, such as newspapers.

The New York City area has been the site of several large-scale studies that are relevant to this study because they focus on Spanish language use and attitudes toward language in Puerto Rican communities. In the first major study, Joshua Fishman and a team of investigators (Fishman et al., 1971) collected data through the use of questionnaires and interviews. The analysis of questionnaires administered to high school aged boys lead Fishman to conclude that "domain diglossia" exists for Puerto Ricans. Fishman defines *domain diglossia* as a bilingual situation in which language use is functionally distinguished. In the community Fishman studies, Spanish is reported to be used in the domains of the family and friendship, whereas English is predominant in the domains of education and employment. One of the problems of this research is that Fishman generalizes about the behavior of an entire community based on findings generated from high school boys. Also problematic is the fact that code-switching, or use of both English and Spanish, was not an option presented on the questionnaire. The survey conducted for this book corrects for these problems by including subjects from different generations and always providing the option of reporting use of both languages on all language related questions.

In 1982, LPTF at the Centro de Estudios Puertorriqueños published a case study of 13 households in East Harlem. The project combined ethnographic and quantitative methodologies to explore language use among 16 children from the ages of 6 to 12 in the home, school, and at play. The LPTF also examined the language attitudes of the parents of the children. They posit a situation of stable bilingualism without diglossia. They find that both languages are used in all domains, although Spanish or English predominates in certain situations or for certain speech events. Language choice is different for the various age groups (LPTF, 1982). For children, language choice depends on sex, peer involvement, and activities. Observing children over a 2-year period, the

LPTF found that boys tend to use more English, whereas girls more frequently speak Spanish and code-switch. Girls demonstrate a greater bilingual ability (LPTF, 1982). Adolescents seem to rely mostly on English, and adults usually speak Spanish. Although examining similar issues, my study benefits from a much larger sample size.

BRENTWOOD LANGUAGE USE
AND ATTITUDE SURVEY

The survey I distributed attempts to gauge patterns of Spanish and English language use, as well as attitudes about the importance of the two languages in the community, and various language phenomena such as code-mixing. The survey has 50 items evenly divided between open-ended questions and directed questions (see appendix). It is two pages long and is printed in English on one side and in Spanish on the other side. Two versions of the questionnaire were produced, one for students and one for parents. They differed only with respect to a few questions that are group specific (such as the language spoken to children/parents).

I obtained a list of Hispanic-surnamed students from the Brentwood School District and distributed the questionnaire to students on that list in January 1991. In that month, the Brentwood School District reported that out of 11,423 students in the district, 39% were Latinos. The survey was handed out to all Hispanic-surnamed students in the high school (11th and 12th grades), the 10th grade center, two junior high schools (7th and 8th grades), and two elementary schools (5th and 6th grades) with high Latino populations. Each student received a packet with a questionnaire for the student and two questionnaires for the parents or care takers, a short letter explaining the purpose of the survey, and a consent form for the parents to sign to allow their child to participate in the study. The packets were handed to the students during homeroom and they were instructed to return them within the week. One thousand five hundred packets were distributed. Of these, 200 were returned without being filled out because the student was not in class (either because she or he had moved or left school) or because the child was not Hispanic; 500 questionnaires were returned but many of these were only partly completed. I analyzed the 371 questionnaires that were completely filled out; of these 151 are student surveys and 220 are adult surveys.

DEMOGRAPHIC CHARACTERISTICS
OF ADULT SAMPLE

The majority of the adult respondents, 55%, self-identified as Puerto Rican. Of these, 42% were born in Puerto Rico and 13% were born in New York to Puerto Rican parents. Other Latinos in the sample include:

Salvadoreans, 11%; Dominicans, 10%; Guatemalans, 10%, and Colombians, 5%. Groups that appeared in the sample in smaller numbers accounted for the other 9% of respondents. These included people from Honduras, Ecuador, Uruguay, Mexico, Costa Rica, Nicaragua, Peru, and Cuba. These figures confirm what many observers have noted, namely that the composition of the Latino community on Long Island is rapidly changing. A profile of Hispanic households in Suffolk County conducted in 1980 (Rosenberg, 1981) found that 78.2% identified as Puerto Rican. In the 1990s this figure dropped to 60%. Clearly, the major influx of Latinos into the Long Island region has come from Central and South America, but Puerto Ricans continue to compose the largest Latino subgroup in Brentwood and they have a long and established history. Latino cultural, social, and political life in Brentwood continues to be dominated by Puerto Ricans (see chap. 1). In the following sections, I discuss the results of the surveys answered by Puerto Ricans.

The Puerto Rican adult group has the following characteristics: 60% have lived on Long Island 10 years or more; 25% have been in Brentwood for more than 20 years. Sixteen percent have completed more than a high school education. Sixty-seven percent of the respondents hold blue collar jobs; 23% hold white collar jobs; and the rest work at home or are retired. The greater proportion of the Puerto Rican respondents, 42%, were between 31 and 40 years of age, while 34% were between 41 and 50. Forty-two percent of the respondents are male and 58% are female.

DEMOGRAPHIC CHARACTERISTICS
OF STUDENT SAMPLE

The students completed 151 questionnaires. Sixty-seven percent of the respondents were born in the United States (includes all Puerto Ricans), and 33% were born in other countries. Seventy-four questionnaires were answered by Puerto Ricans, 48 by students from countries with more than a 5% response rate (Dominican Republic, El Salvador, and Guatemala), and 29 were completed by other students that did not fall in these two categories (students from Colombia, Honduras, Ecuador, Nicaragua, or Uruguay). Of the 74 Puerto Rican students who responded to the survey, 85% were born in New York, and 15% were born in Puerto Rico. Thirty-seven percent were in 5th or 6th grade, 25% were in 7th to 9th grade, and 38% were in 10th to 12th grade. The majority, 60%, were between the ages of 11 and 15; 27% were between 16 and 20; and the rest, 13%, were 10 or under.

ADULT LANGUAGE USE

If minority language is maintained at all in the United States, it is in the home domain where it tends to survive the longest. In Brentwood, the results of the survey indicate that Spanish is reported being spoken less than English by Puerto Rican adults outside the home, but that it is the preferred language when speaking with spouses and parents. However, when speaking with friends, workmates, and job superiors, English is the favored language. Important in terms of cross-generational language maintenance is the fact that with children, parents state they are most likely to speak both Spanish and English.[1]

As Fig. 2.1 demonstrates, in the case of language used to converse with a spouse, 49% of the adult Puerto Ricans report speaking exclusively in Spanish to their spouses and approximately 40% use this language to speak with their siblings. As is to be expected, more than 70% use Spanish as the language of communication with their parents. However, with their children, only 20% of the Puerto Ricans speak exclusively in Spanish, whereas 38% use both languages to speak to them. Many Puerto Ricans, 42%, speak to their children exclusively in English. Because the amount of Spanish input in the home probably has most to do with maintenance of Spanish as a home language, we would

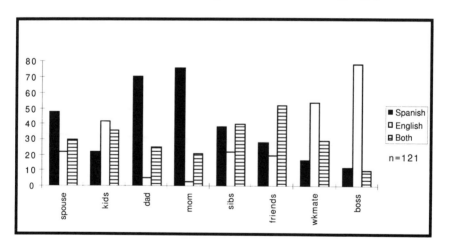

FIG. 2.1.   Puerto Rican parent language usage.

[1]When asked which language(s) they speak with others, respondents could indicate Spanish, English, or both (see question seven of the language use survey in the appendix). For the purposes of this analysis, the crucial question is how much Spanish is being spoken. It is not relevant if respondents interpret this question to mean code-switching in individual conversations or use of either language across conversations. Questions 15 to 21, on the other hand, specifically address code-switching behavior.

expect to see that the amount of Spanish spoken by the parents has direct repercussions in the rates of Spanish spoken by the children. This is analyzed in the next section.

In their conversations with friends and workmates, only 20% of the Puerto Ricans speak exclusively in Spanish, whereas 50% converse in both languages. Not surprisingly, in work situations with "the boss" English language use predominates.

STUDENT LANGUAGE USE

The results in Puerto Rican adult language use are echoed and magnified in the children's language use in terms of the preference for English in some contexts. The students use some Spanish with their parents and primarily English with everyone else. As can be seen from Fig. 2.2, the Puerto Rican students report speaking considerably less Spanish than their parents. Only 20% to 30% of the Puerto Rican students speak Spanish exclusively to their parents. Forty percent of the Puerto Rican children speak English to their fathers, whereas 35% speak English to their mothers. However, it is important to underscore the number of students who choose both Spanish and English to communicate with their parents. Between 35% and 40% reported that they use both languages when speaking with their parents. This suggests that the home is neither an exclusively Spanish nor English domain. This also suggests that Spanish is still commonly heard and spoken in the home by children and parents; it has not been completely lost.

The report that children use mostly English when speaking to their parents is not surprising because, as we have previously seen, the Puerto Rican parents apparently use mostly English, or speak both languages, with their children. Also according to the survey, when speaking to their siblings, close to 60% of the Puerto Rican students speak exclusively in English. Students claim to speak mostly English to their friends and classmates as well. These results indicate that in the home environment of the Brentwood Puerto Rican there is considerably less Spanish language use than English language use when youngsters speak among themselves.

ADULT LANGUAGE PROFICIENCY

Determining language proficiency is difficult, regardless of how one tries to measure it. Self-reporting proficiency, for example, is a subjective matter dependent on the speaker's point of reference. As García et al. (1988) suggest, uneducated speakers who have a functional ability in a language, that is, they can write letters, read signs, applications, and

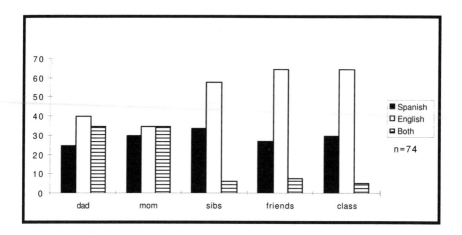

FIG. 2.2.   Puerto Rican student language usage.

popular magazines, might judge their proficiency in a language to be
very good. Educated persons, who are measuring their proficiency
against an academic norm might, on the other hand, underestimate
their proficiency. Another complicating factor is the stigmatization at-
tached to some Spanish varieties. It is well documented that the Caribbean dialects are the most stigmatized of the Spanish dialects, even
among Caribbean speakers themselves (LPTF, 1982). In the Brentwood
community, Puerto Rican adults and children differ in their assessment
of their own level of comfort with the languages in their repertoire. In
both cases, their proficiency with the respective languages is related to
their overall use of the languages. Sixty percent of Puerto Rican adults
claim to be bilingual (i.e., they speak, read, and write both languages).
For 45%, Spanish is their best language, whereas 18% state that English
is their best language, and 37% are equally comfortable with both
languages. That the majority of the adults claim to be bilingual corresponds to the reported widespread use of the two languages, as reported
in Fig. 2.1.

STUDENT LANGUAGE PROFICIENCY

Eighty-one percent of the Puerto Rican students say they are bilingual.
Eighteen percent of them speak only English. When asked to identify
their best language, the majority, 62%, report English; only 22% are
comfortable with both equally. Fourteen percent of the Puerto Rican
students are most comfortable with Spanish.
    There is a shift in Spanish language use and proficiency across
generations. Although bilingualism is the norm for both parents and

children, in the parents' cases, Spanish is favored, whereas in the students', English is preferred. All students report speaking less Spanish compared to their parents. Although more than 80% of all students claim to be bilingual, in terms of overall language use, Spanish is used much less by the children. Puerto Rican children use much more English than their parents and feel more confident about their English. The results suggest that parents are accommodating to their children's language preference by speaking to them in English or using both languages, even though the parents themselves are more comfortable speaking in Spanish. However, in homes where grandparents live or are frequently present, a bilingualism that favors Spanish is the norm.

Although the data presented here can be interpreted as indicating that language shift is underway, it is important to consider the ethnographic evidence that suggests that as children become young adults their linguistic behavior may change depending on their networks and associations. As the LPTF (1980) documents for a Puerto Rican community in New York City, a "life cycle" of language change (p. 29) may be operating, whereby very young children speak primarily Spanish until adolescence when they begin to prefer English. However, as they become adults and are integrated into Spanish-speaking adult networks, their use of Spanish increases. I observed this same process in the Brentwood community, where young adults were consciously trying to reactivate their Spanish—because of church attendance, mate selection, community activism, or the like (see chap. 1). The survey data offer a snapshot of a particular moment in the life cycle of language change. But as the ethnographic information suggests, what emerges is not the whole picture.

ADULT CODE-MIXING BEHAVIOR AND ATTITUDES

I also inquired about code-mixing behavior and attitudes toward mixing. Code-mixing, the alternation of two languages in a single utterance, is common in Spanish–English bilingual communities in the United States, as well as in other multilingual situations. Despite research that asserts that code-mixing is a natural process in certain bilingual situations (Grosjean, 1982), and studies (Poplack, 1982a) that suggest that those who engage in intrasentential switching are the most balanced bilinguals in the speech community, many bilinguals and educators in Spanish-speaking communities continue to think that code-mixing indicates a lack of dominance in one or both languages, or is a sign of laziness. A number of studies (Kachru, 1985; Torres, 1992a) explore code-mixing in discourse and detail the creative functions this phenomenon can have, but community members themselves often do not share this particular perspective. Despite these negative assessments, speakers continue to code-mix for a variety of reasons, from the sociopsychological, such as intergroup solidarity and identification (Fernández, 1990), to the linguistic, such as to fill lexical gaps (Silva-Corvalán, 1983a; Torres, 1992a).

When asked in the survey whether they code-mix, 82% of the Puerto Rican adults state that they do. When asked what they thought about mixing, 24% of the Puerto Ricans on Long Island chose the response "it is good," whereas 39% say "it is bad," and 36% say they "don't know." A follow-up open ended question asked respondents how they felt about code-mixing. The majority who think that code-mixing is a problem indicated reasons such as linguistic deficiency, "*es malo porque no hablan bien ninguno de los dos idiomas*," ["it is bad because they don't speak either language well."] Others considered the practice negative yet still recognized its contextual usefulness, "It isn't right but we do it at times to keep others out of our conversations." And some respondents voiced very positive feelings about code-mixing, "We are combining the best of both worlds."

Another open-ended question in the Brentwood survey asked the respondents why they code-mixed. Answers were grouped in categories. Figure 2.3 shows how both Puerto Rican parents and students responded.

The results indicate that code-mixing is a familiar behavior to the Puerto Rican adults. Most Puerto Rican adults (48%) say they mix codes because it is a habit, whereas 24% claim they switch when they do not know a word in the language they are speaking; 18% mix because of the context, in other words, as one respondent stated, "in order to better communicate with others" in their bilingual community.

Respondents were also asked if their children engage in code-mixing and whether they tried to censor this behavior. Seventy-three percent

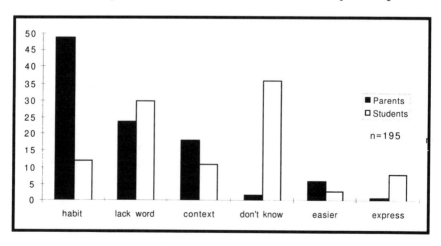

FIG. 2.3. Reasons for mixing.

of the Puerto Rican adults report that their children code-mix and 29% tell their children not to switch between English and Spanish.

Responses suggest that, although most Puerto Rican adults code-mix, many still see it as a stigmatized behavior. It is a linguistic behavior that Puerto Ricans have long been exposed to and engage in but about which they are still ambivalent. Many feel that code-mixing is a sign of linguistic problems. For example, one respondent writes that he mixes "because I get confused and say it the way it comes out." Another respondent states that she mixes, "because of mixed thought patterns." Others claim mixing is natural given the bilingual context where, "if the people you are talking to speak both languages then it doesn't matter," or "because I'm always together with people that mix it."

STUDENT CODE-MIXING BEHAVIOR
AND ATTITUDES

Seventy-seven percent of the students state that they code-mix. Their feelings about mixing are similar to their parents'. Eighteen percent of the Puerto Ricans agree that code-mixing is good; 35% of the Puerto Ricans agree that it is bad; and most students, 47%, say that they do not know if it is good or bad (see Fig. 2.3).

Most students thus say that they do not know why they code-mix. Thirty percent think that they do so because they lack a word in the language they start speaking. Almost 10% of the Puerto Rican students claim that they code-mix to express themselves better. One student writes that he mixes "because it sounds nice and some friends understand better." Another states, "when I get mad or happy it helps me say what I want."

Overall, both Puerto Rican parents and students are somewhat critical of code-mixing behavior. They understand that it is one of the reasons that their speech is stigmatized. However ambivalent their feelings are about this linguistic practice, code-mixing is a characteristic trait in the speech of many Brentwood Puerto Ricans. As we see in the analysis of narratives (chaps. 3 and 4), code-mixing functions differently in the speech of different community members.

ADULT ATTITUDES ABOUT LANGUAGE
AND THEIR CHILDREN

The questionnaire also sought to gauge how the participants evaluate the function of Spanish and English in their children's lives. Most parents feel that it is important that their children learn both Spanish and English. Ninety-three percent of the Puerto Ricans think it is important that their children learn Spanish. Ninety-eight percent feel that learning English is important to their children.

In an open-ended question parents were asked to state why they felt learning Spanish and English was important to their children. Overwhelmingly, most Puerto Ricans name affective reasons for learning Spanish. More than 50% of Puerto Ricans agree that Spanish is valuable because it is part of the children's cultural heritage. One parent expresses it this way, *"porque es una pérdida que los padres hablen español y los hijos pierdan esta oportunidad para aprender otra lengua. También es parte de la familia."* ["because it is a loss that the parents speak Spanish and the children lose this opportunity to speak another language. Also it is part of the family."] The second most frequently given reason is a statement to the effect that speaking more than one language is beneficial, although, in most cases respondents do not state why this is so.

On the other hand, more than 50% feel that their children should learn English because it is the language of the United States. Other parents also point out the importance of independence that comes from speaking the majority language of the country, "They don't have to depend on anybody to speak for them because they can defend themselves without depending on anyone else to speak for them." Another parent is more direct in stating why English is important for the children, *"Si aprenden inglés se defienden mejor de los que nos atacan en contra de nuestro idioma."* ["If they learn English they can defend themselves better from those who attack us against our language."]

Almost 10% say that English is vital for their children's future and specifically for employment. Some answers suggest that parents are basing their desires for their children's linguistic development on the hardships that their generation has endured because of language problems. One respondent writes, "In this country you have to speak English, or you will suffer discrimination to the point of being offered only low paying jobs, and so on." Another states, "English is important for employment. Speaking fluent English tends to brake [sic] some discrimination barriers."

Finally, parents were asked who should bear responsibility for teaching Spanish to their children. The majority of the Puerto Ricans, 83%, feel that the responsibility should be shared by both the family and the schools. Fifteen percent of the Puerto Ricans think it is solely the family's responsibility, and no one claims that the schools should be entirely responsible for teaching the children Spanish.

These results indicate that Puerto Rican parents believe that it is important that their children speak both Spanish and English. Whereas they declare different reasons for valuing the two languages, bilingualism is certainly what they prefer for their children.

LANGUAGE ATTITUDES OF THE STUDENTS

Students were also asked their opinions concerning the role of Spanish and English in their lives. Eighty-nine percent of the Puerto Rican students claim that it is important for them to speak Spanish. Ninety-nine percent claim the same about English. As with their parents, the reasons given for the value of Spanish have more to do with affective than instrumental factors. Most students respond that Spanish is important for cultural reasons, related to their heritage or that of their parents. To an open-ended question inquiring why it is important to speak Spanish, one student writes, "because I am Puerto Rican and I should know how to speak it because all Puerto Ricans should speak Spanish." The second most popular response is that it is necessary to know Spanish in order to communicate with family members and friends who do not speak English. One student wrote, "because if I don't speak Spanish I wouldn't be able to speak with my family." These responses are similar to the parents' answers when asked why it is important that the children learn Spanish.

The most frequently given reason by students for the importance of English is that it is the language of the United States. A student put it this way: "People in the U.S. speak English. In this world if you don't speak it you need someone to speak for you, I would rather speak for myself."

Ten percent of the Puerto Rican adults also say that English is a universal language, whereas no students make such a claim about English; nor do the students identify Spanish as *the* language or even *a* language of the United States. Eight percent of the Puerto Rican students also state that English is important for educational reasons, meaning that schools teach in English so they must know the language. Although 40% of the Puerto Rican students have had at least 1 year of bilingual education or classes in ESL, fewer than 10% of the students identify Spanish as important for education.

Like their parents, the students appreciate the value of being bilingual. They also tend to attach different values to the languages in their linguistic repertoire, but they overwhelmingly report that both Spanish and English are important in their lives.

ATTITUDES ON HISPANIC LIFE ON LONG ISLAND

A series of questions in the Long Island survey tried to assess general attitudes about Latino life and language on Long Island. The results of this part of the survey reveal that, for Puerto Rican parents and students, the Spanish language is not defined as *the* crucial ingredient that constitutes Latino identity. The respondents do indicate that Spanish is alive and well in Long Island. But aside from language, close to 70% of all respondents agree that the Spanish culture is being maintained on Long Island.

Many participants express the view that Hispanics on Long Island suffer discrimination. Fifty-six percent of the Puerto Ricans adults agreed with this statement, whereas 12% did not agree and 32% were undecided. Fewer Puerto Rican students agreed that Hispanics on Long Island suffer discrimination. Thirty-eight percent agreed with the statement, whereas 24% did not and 38% were unsure. In chapter 5, we see that as these students become young adults, they recognize discrimination more readily and are more willing than the older generation to speak out against it.

When asked if Hispanics on Long Island suffer discrimination because of language, the agreement rate rises for both groups. More than 50% of both Puerto Rican adults and students agreed that language discrimination exists in Brentwood.

Several people addressed the issue of discrimination in the area in the survey allotted for comments. One adult writes, "The question about discrimination it does not only apply to language but also because of skin color and attitude." Another writes, "*Siempre hay discriminación en contra de los hispanos de Brentwood aunque estemos bien preparados educacionalmente.*" ["There is always discrimination against Hispanics even when we are well-prepared educationally."] On the other hand, another Puerto Rican adult expresses that "anyone who live [sic] here should learn English. If not go back to where they come from." In general however, the majority of the Puerto Rican adults feel that Hispanics on Long Island face discrimination, and both adults and children overwhelmingly concur that Hispanics face discrimination because of language problems.

Interestingly, several women addressed the issue of sexual discrimination in the part of the survey where they were invited to add other comments. One woman writes, "*¿Por qué no hay preguntas sobre la discriminación en contra las latinas? Sufrimos mucho por el machismo en nuestra comunidad.*" ["Why aren't there any questions about discrimination against latinas? We suffer a lot because of machismo in our community."] Another young woman adds, "The worst discrimination I face is not about language but about guys who think girls should stay home while they are free to come and go." The issues of racism and sexism are taken up again in chapter 5.

GENDER ANALYSIS

Few studies focus on gender and language choice in U.S. Puerto Rican communities. The LPTF (1982) study finds that boys speak mostly English, whereas girls more frequently use Spanish or both Spanish and

English. Pedraza (1987) observes that although women's networks in the Puerto Rican community, sometimes use both languages, they prefer Spanish. Zentella (1987) offers a sociological explanation to account for the fact that girls speak more Spanish, than boys in the New York Puerto Rican community. She argues that as girls and boys are socialized to assume their gender roles, girls are exposed to more Spanish and they are expected to respond in Spanish. They are in the home around the mostly Spanish-speaking women more frequently than are the boys. They are depended on to take care of younger siblings, help fulfill household tasks, such as cooking and sewing, and they must attend church services with the women. They also watch the Spanish soap operas with the women in the family and other friends. As a result of their participation in these gender-specific activities, girls receive Spanish input and speak the home language more frequently than their male peers.[2]

Analysis of the results of reported language use by sex in the Brentwood community indicate that generalizations concerning male and female differences without a consideration of generation are untenable; each age group has its own patterns. Although we would expect to see that the students follow the adult patterns, this does not occur. Although a higher percentage of Puerto Rican male adults report speaking exclusively Spanish (compare Figs. 2.4 and 2.5), in the student sample a higher percentage of females speak exclusively Spanish compared to the males (Figs. 2.6 and 2.7).

Figures 2.4 and 2.5 present the Puerto Rican male and female language use responses for adults. In the adult group, fewer women than

---

[2]There are also several studies that analyze language use and gender in Mexican-American communities. For example, Patella and Kuvlesky (1973) investigate the language choice of rural-dwelling high school students from a low socioeconomic background. They notice a shift from Spanish to English for both sexes as the situational context moves from private settings (home, neighborhood) to public settings (school, workplace). Males use Spanish more with parents and close friends; in these situations, females prefer English. However, females prefer to read literature in Spanish whereas male prefer English language literature. Solé (1978) researches language use among urban dwelling Mexican-American college students. She does not find sex-differentiated behavior in interactions with grandparents (Spanish) and in educational or work situations (English). However, in all other interaction situations, for example with parents, older and younger relatives, and neighbors, Solé identifies a consistent pattern of males' speaking Spanish and code-mixing, and females' speaking more English. This pattern also obtains when considering *subvocal speech*, the language used for prayer, daydreaming, and the releasing of both positive and negative strong emotions.

Both Solé (1978) and Patella and Kuvlesky (1973) refer to Mexican American cultural and sociopsychological factors to account for observed differences. Solé reasons, for example, that Mexican American females use English as a reaction against Latino cultural role limitations and expectations. She argues that Mexican American women more readily assimilate to Anglo culture and language because they think that Anglo culture will offer them more opportunities for socioeconomic and personal success.

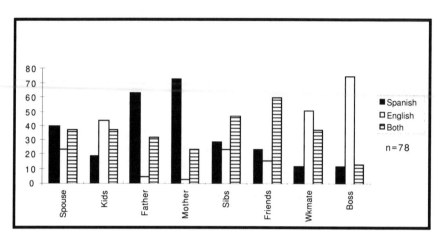

FIG. 2.4.   Puerto Rican female adult language usage.

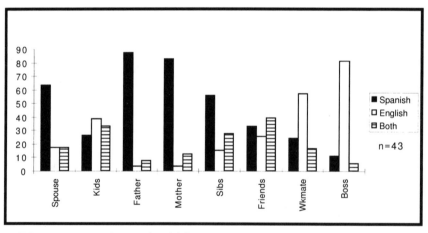

FIG. 2.5.   Puerto Rican male adult language usage.

men seem to be speaking Spanish. Forty-one percent of the women speak exclusively Spanish with their spouses, whereas 63% of the males do so. With children, 19% of the females and 27% of the males speak exclusively in Spanish. Most parents use English when speaking to their children, although more women speak to them exclusively in English. When speaking to brothers and sisters, again a higher percentage of men (56%) than women (29%) speak only in Spanish. Most females (47%) speak both languages to siblings. With friends, a difference between men and women is also noted: Fifty-nine percent of the women use both languages, whereas for men, only 40%, also speak both; but more men (34%) than women (24%) speak only Spanish with friends.

Given these figures it is not surprising to learn that only 41% of the women and 51% of the males say that Spanish is their best language.

With the Puerto Rican students a surprisingly different pattern results. Figures 2.6 and 2.7 indicate that slightly more Puerto Rican female students than males are using Spanish overall, especially when we consider nonfamily members.

About 25% to 30% of both males and female students speak Spanish to their parents. Male Puerto Rican students never report speaking Spanish to siblings, whereas 8% of the females say they do. On the other hand, 45% of the males and only 29% of the females speak both English and Spanish with their siblings. With friends and classmates, the males

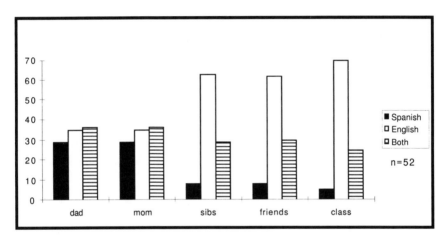

FIG. 2.6.   Puerto Rican female student usage.

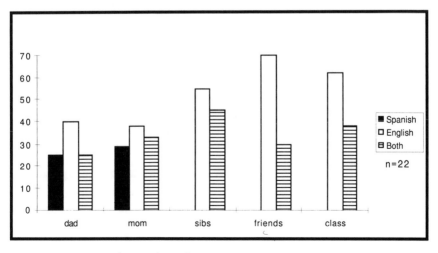

FIG. 2.7.   Puerto Rican male student usage.

in this group apparently never speak Spanish, whereas between 5% to 10% of the females say they speak Spanish to friends and classmates.

Because a higher percentage of females (24%) than males, (18%), identify Spanish as their best language, it is understandable that females would more frequently speak exclusively in Spanish as the foregoing data indicate. Most of the Puerto Rican students (63% of the females and 68% of the males) say that English is their best language; whereas 14% of both genders report that they are equally comfortable in both languages.

As can be seen, it is difficult to generalize about gender differences and language use across generations. For all Puerto Rican students, English predominates, although females seem to be maintaining Spanish at a slightly higher rate than their male counterparts. This is occurring despite the fact that Puerto Rican female parents are using more English than male parents. Interestingly, it is with friends and classmates that the greatest difference is noted between male and female students. The female students are apparently forming networks with others who continue to use Spanish outside the home.

This complex picture challenges gender-specific sociocultural explanations of the type offered by Zentella (1987). Whereas parental linguistic behavior heavily impacts the linguistic behavior of preschool children, as children interact with peers outside the school, their speech and language use patterns are influenced by another range of linguistic behaviors. Therefore, to explain gender differences it is helpful to consider the ethnographic data (chap. 1). In Brentwood, I observed that more young females are involved in Spanish-speaking churches and clubs in schools than are young males. In this case, activities outside the home aid in the maintenance of the Spanish language for females. Network participation seems to be a strong predictor of language preference and use.

CONCLUSION

The survey leads me to conclude that bilingualism currently predominates for Brentwood Puerto Rican residents. The linguistic repertoire of the Puerto Rican parents and students surveyed includes Spanish and English to differing degrees. In terms of both language use and attitudes, for the majority of all respondents, adults and children alike, Spanish continues to be highly valued. The Puerto Ricans, overall, are using both Spanish and English, or exclusively English, more frequently than Spanish in most contexts and with most interlocutors. However, the Brentwood Puerto Rican students are most comfortable with English.

The survey thus offers a snapshot of the present dynamics of language use patterns in the community, but does not present the whole picture. The ethnographic data suggest that if youngsters do not remain in situations where they are in contact with parents and other family members who are Spanish-dominant, and actually speak the language at home and in other contexts, the likelihood that they will continue to use Spanish diminishes. However, if they continue to move in familial and work situations where they receive frequent Spanish input and use the language, their comfort level with Spanish increases. The ethnographic data on young people as they leave high school indicate that as young adults participate in networks where Spanish predominates, such as the church, certain work situations, and political groups, the patterns suggested in the survey are reversed for some speakers.

Nonetheless, Puerto Rican young people are hearing and speaking less Spanish than English. Given that the Puerto Rican parents frequently use both languages themselves, communication between these two generations often takes place using two codes. However, there are situations where young people are called on to speak primarily in Spanish, for example, in the not uncommon situation of interacting with monolingual relatives.

Among other linguistic skills that they possess, young people can and do participate in informal storytelling activities in Spanish. The next two chapters consider how the reduced exposure and use of the home language affect Spanish structure in the specific context of narrative performance.

3

Narrative Structure

INTRODUCTION

In the previous chapter we saw that, for Puerto Ricans of all age groups in Brentwood, the Spanish language is not exclusively used in the home. Many speakers use both Spanish and English, and others, especially the young use much English. In this chapter, I examine the Spanish language narratives of Spanish-dominant, bilingual, and English-dominant Puerto Rican speakers for evidence of language loss or simplification. I analyze the stories of these three groups of Puerto Rican speakers and conclude that, despite a situation where Spanish is used less often than in a monolingual context, the Spanish narratives of English-dominant speakers (Group 3) are as well developed at the levels of narrative structure, the verb system, and syntactic complexity as are the narratives of Spanish-dominant (Group 1) and bilingual speakers (Group 2). When the Spanish narratives of speakers of different generations are compared from the point of view of structure and grammar, the narratives are more similar than different. This analysis extends the perspective in the previous chapter by emphasizing the rich Spanish language ability of all three groups of Puerto Rican Spanish speakers in the Brentwood community.

The trend in much of the literature on Spanish in the United States is to use the language data of successive generations of U.S. Latino speakers to advance theories of language loss and simplification (Silva-Corvalán, 1986, 1988, 1994). In contrast, my study of Brentwood Puerto Rican Spanish narratives follows in the tradition of Labov's (1972) studies of narratives in Black and White communities. Labov compares oral narratives of Black speakers to those of White speakers and finds that although there are differences, the narratives of the Black speakers are not impoverished. In fact, "the Black vernacular is the vehicle of communication used by some of the most talented and effective speakers of the English language" (Labov, 1972, p. 396). Similarly, I contend that the narratives of my three groups of Puerto Ricans, those who are Spanish-dominant, bilingual, and English-dominant, are structurally sound and in no way deficient.

In order to carry out this analysis, I compare my Brentwood Puerto Rican data to studies of narratives produced in monolingual Spanish speaking contexts (Silva-Corvalán, 1983b) and to other studies of narratives produced by different generations of U.S. Spanish speakers in other communities. Silva-Corvalán, in a number of provocative studies (1986, 1988, 1990), identifies stages of loss of tense, mood, and aspect in the verb system of Los Angeles Mexican American Spanish speakers. In an analysis of narratives across three generations of Los Angeles Mexican Americans, Silva-Corvalán (1988) documents simplification in the narrative structure and discourse strategies of the stories delivered by successive generational groups. In another study based on the same Los Angeles data, Gutiérrez (1990) identifies a simplification process occurring at the level of clause complexity in oral narratives. I argue that although the same type of processes might be expected in the Brentwood Puerto Rican case, because it is a language contact situation in which Spanish is used less and less in successive generations, an analysis of the narratives leads to a different conclusion, namely that the structural and syntactic integrity of Spanish is maintained. This type of analysis is important, as Labov (1972) states, "The most useful service which linguists can perform today is to clear away the illusion of verbal deprivation and to provide a more adequate notion of the relations between standard and nonstandard dialects" (p. 202).

VERB USE AND NARRATIVE STRUCTURE

In this section I argue that, despite a difference in Spanish language proficiency at the level of narrative structure, all Brentwood Puerto Ricans in my sample produce narratives that are well developed and that exhibit the appropriate range of verbs and verb forms expected for the type of narratives offered. There are some differences in the production of the narratives across the three groups. Spanish-dominant speakers rely on the present tense more so than the other two groups and the English-dominant speakers use more English in their narratives. However, all speakers produce dynamic and rich stories in Spanish.

Stories produced by speakers with different migration and acquisition histories offer a unique database from which to study and compare the narrative strategies and verb usage employed by different members of the bilingual community. Narratives of personal experience have a uniform structure and a familiar, recurrent organization. As we see, certain grammatical and discourse features are associated with specific narrative components (Silva-Corvalán, 1983b). Different kinds of narratives of past experience are possible, including those that recount general events of the past, or those that narrate events that happened to family members or friends. For this analysis, I considered 10 narratives from each generational group. For purposes of comparability, I selected narratives that describe one event in the past in which the narrator is the central participant.

In their conversations with me, community members all produced well-formed narratives. All participants generated stories that consist of more than what Labov (1972) defines as a *minimal narrative*, a sequence of two clauses that are temporally ordered. The stories chosen for analysis are more fully developed than this, consisting of many of the components that are said to characterize narratives (Labov, 1972): an abstract, orientation, complicating actions, evaluation, resolution, and coda (see the introductory chapter for a definition of these terms). Not all of the Puerto Rican narratives contain each of these elements; some elements are optional (Labov, 1972). Because the narratives analyzed here are extracted from longer conversations between the participants and me, it is not suprising that they do not all contain abstracts and codas. The functions of these components could be addressed in terms of the overall conversation rather than in the narrative itself. However, all the narratives include at least an orientation, complicating actions, and an evaluation component; about one third of all narratives also contain an abstract and a coda.

The following narrative (Text 3-A) produced by a 17-year-old, female, English-dominant speaker (Group 3) is used to exemplify these components. In this narrative the woman tells a gripping story about a time she and her friend narrowly escaped being raped. This narrative has an abstract (lines 1–4), which summarizes what is to follow; an orientation section follows (lines 5–12), which introduces the participants and describes the setting. In the rest of the narrative, evaluative clauses, where the speaker comments on the story (lines 19, 24–26, 28–34), are interspersed with complicating action clauses that advance the action of the story (lines 13–18, 20–23, 27, 35–39). A resolution, which wraps up the story, concludes the narrative in lines 40–41.

Text 3-A

I: *¿No te daba miedo estar en el tren a las cinco de la manaña?*
        No, no I don't know, *no me daba miedo porque yo estaba acostumbrá*

I: *¿Nunca te molestaron?*

1)   *Un día nos cogieron a mí y a C.*
2)   *y nos llevaron a un hotel*
3)   and they tied us up

I: *¿Qué?*

4)   and I thought they were going to rape us
5)   yeah, *yo conocía a este moreno*
6)   *después que introdució a su esposa*

7)   *pueh despuéh sabe nos llevaron para su casa*
8)   *allí 'ta bien* you know
9)   *yo hablé con la esposa*
10)   *so la esposa me dijo,*
11)   "you know take the ride with them
12)   you know they'll drop you off where you want to go"
13)   *entonceh noh fuimoh a cenar*
14)   *entonce yo,* "hold it
15)   *yo tengo que ir pa' casa*
16)   *porque yo tengo que ir pa' la 'cuela mañana"*
17)   *dijo, "no tú no puedeh ir pa' tu casa"*
18)   *yo, "no, yo voy pa' casa"*
19)   you know we was like please take me home
20)   *"no, no hasta que tú nos des un canto"*
21)   I said, "what?"
22)   *"hasta que nos des un canto"*
23)   *y grité*
24)   C. was a virgin at the time
25)   C. said, "what?, Oh my God!"
26)   C. got hysterical
27)   *entonceh yo le dije*
28)   *"mira, yo no entiendo porque tú estás haciendo eso*
29)   *porque tú eres tan feo*
30)   *que no puedeh encontrar a nadie que te dé un canto*
31)   *tú tieneh los dienteh amarillo*
32)   *y te apesta la boca o-*
33)   *y me vas a tener que matar"*
34)   C. was like shut up you are making things worse
35)   *y entonceh llegaron un montón de negroh*
36)   *y dijeron,* "party time"
37)   *yo dije,* "party time, oh my God!"
38)   *dehpuéh vino un moreno*
39)   *y dijo, "suéltenla"*
40)   *y noh soltaron por* Jones Beach
41)   *y tuvimoh que andar de* Jones Beach *acá*

[I: Weren't you afraid to be on the train at five in the morning?
       No, no I don't know, I wasn't afraid because I was used to it
I: You were never bothered?

1)   One day they took me and C.
2)   and they took us to a hotel
3)   and they tied us up
I: What?

4)   and I thought they were going to rape us
5)   yeah, I knew this Black guy
6)   after he introduced his wife
7)   well after you know they took us to their house
8)   there, it's all right y'know
9)   I talked with the wife
10)   so the wife told me,
11)   "y'know take the ride with them,
12)   y'know they'll drop you off where you want to go"
13)   then well we went to eat
14)   then me, "hold it
15)   I have to go home
16)   because I have to go to school tomorrow"
17)   he said, "no you can't go to your house"
18)   me, "no I'm going to my house"
19)   you know we was like please take me home
20)   "no, not until you give us a piece"
21)   I said, "what?"
22)   "until you give us a piece"
23)   and I screamed
24)   C. was a virgin at the time
25)   C. said, "What, oh my God!"
26)   C. got hysterical
27)   then I said to him,
28)   "look I don't understand why you are doing this
29)   because you are so ugly
30)   that you can't find no one to give you a piece
31)   you have yellow teeth
32)   and your mouth stinks o-
33)   and you are gonna have to kill me"
34)   C. was like shut up you are making things worse
35)   and then a bunch of Black guys arrived
36)   and they said, "party time"
37)   I said, "party time, oh my god!"
38)   then a Black guy came
39)   and said, "let them go"
40)   and they let us go by Jones Beach
41)   and we had to walk here from Jones Beach]

The most common tenses used in narratives of personal experience are the preterite, imperfect and present tenses. The function of these tenses are exemplified later in the context of Text 3-A. In general, each verb tense has a general meaning that can be more specifically defined according to its use in context. For example, the present tense (*tá* [it is]) is used to express an event that may co-occur with the moment of speaking with no further temporal specifications (line 8). The historical present (*tengo que* [have to], *eres* [you are], *puedes* [can], *tienes* [have], *te apesta* [it stinks]) is commonly used in the narrative in order to give a sense of immediacy, as if the actions are being relived at the moment of speech (lines 15, 16, 29–32). The preterite (*nos cogieron / nos llevaron* [they took us], *nos soltaron* [they let us go], *tuvimos* [we had to]) focuses on the beginning or end of an action from a past perspective, or the past event is viewed as a totality (lines 1–2, 40–41). The imperfect *conocía* [I knew] conveys the sense of an ongoing, habitual, or iterative action, again from the perspective of the past (line 5).

As Silva-Corvalán (1983b) notes, specific tenses are more apt to be used in certain components of a narrative due to the function of that section. Similarly, because of the particular function of a section, select meanings of a verb are more likely in each section. The orientation section, for example, provides background for a past event and is frequently narrated in the imperfect. And accordingly, the meaning of the imperfect that is most appropriate is ongoingness in the past rather than, for example, iterative action. In the complicating action sections of the narrative, one expects preterite and historical present forms to predominate since these sections usually consist of a series of actions. The imperfect is also expected in the evaluation section, which in many cases is descriptive. Of course, these are tendencies, not absolutes, as is apparent when actual narratives are studied. For example, in Text 3-A, the orientation section (lines 5–12) contains verbs in the imperfect (line 5), the preterite (lines 6–7, 9–10, 12), and the present tense (lines 8, 11).

The verb distribution of my Puerto Rican narratives is not unlike the verb distribution of Spanish monolingual narratives described by Silva-Corvalán (1983b). More importantly, there are few differences between my Puerto Rican Spanish-dominant, bilingual, and English-dominant narratives. In the Mexican and Chilean narratives Silva-Corvalán (1983b) collected, 70% of all the verbs in the orientation are in the imperfect. In my sample, for all three groups the imperfect is also the form most used (Group 1 = 50%, Group 2 = 45%, Group 3 = 43%) in the orientation sections. In my data, the present tense is also widely used in the orientation by all three groups to set the time and place and especially, to describe the participants in the narratives. What is most relevant for this analysis is that no significant difference across the groups in terms of verb usage in the orientation sections is found. All three groups use the verb forms expected in each narrative section. This suggests that despite proficiency differences, all Puerto Rican speakers share similar rules for producing oral narratives in Spanish.

In the complicating action sequences in all the narratives, the most common tenses are the preterite and the historical present for all groups as would be expected. These two tenses account for more than 70% of all tenses in the narratives of the three groups. In the first generation data, however, the present is the most frequent tense in the complicating action section (48%) followed by the preterite (32%). For the other two groups, the preterite is the most commonly used tense (Group 2 = 43% and Group 3 = 42%), followed by the present tense (Group 2 = 41% and Group 3 = 37%). The difference noted may be explained by the greater use by Group 1 of the historical present to advance their narratives.

Speakers tend to use the historical present as an internal evaluation device because it actualizes the events being recounted (Silva-Corvalán, 1983). In my data, the historical present often occurs at the points in the complicating action sections that are most climactic. Direct speech is also often rendered in the historical present and may be considered an internal evaluation device (as in lines 14–16 and 28–33 in Text 3-A). In the Puerto Rican narratives I examined, the historical present is used across the three groups at a much higher frequency than in the Mexican and Chilean narratives studied by Silva-Corvalán. The Spanish-dominant group in my sample uses the historical present slightly more frequently than the other groups do (Group 1 = 50%, Group 2 = 48%, Group 3 = 44%). These speakers tend to dramatize large portions of their narratives, not just the most climactic happenings, more frequently than the other two groups. For example, in the following excerpt (Text 3-B) from a narrative about her efforts to help her children, a first-generation (Group 1) speaker produces most of the story, not only the direct quotes (lines 2–7) or the climax of the narrative (lines 10–14), in the present tense:

Text 3-B

1) *por las tarde llega mi hija*
2) *"vamos a hacer la tarea"*
3) *"¿sabes hacerla?"*
4) *"sí mami"*
5) *"¿necesitas ayuda?"*
6) *"no mami"*
7) *"¿tienes qué hacer un reporte?"*
8) *a la biblioteca*
9) *y yo voy con ella*
10) *yo me siento*
11) *le busco el libro del reporte*
12) *le doy ideas*
13) *le digo más·o menos como escribirlo*
14) *yo le enseño ese interés*
15) *porque para mí el progreso del niño es mi progreso*

[1] in the evening my daughter arrives

2)   "let's do the homework"
3)   "do you know how to do it?"
4)   "yes mom"
5)   "do you need help?"
6)   "no mom"
7)   "do you have to do a report?"
8)   to the library
9)   and I go with her
10)   and I sit
11)   I look for the book for the report
12)   I give her ideas
13)   I tell her more or less what to write
14)   I show her interest
15)   because for me the child's progress is my progress]

However, all three groups seem to use the historical present regularly in order to dramatize key portions of the complicating actions as well as to express direct speech. In Text 3-A, produced by an English-dominant speaker, the narrator uses direct speech (lines 14–22) to express a very dramatic part of her story, the point where she learns that the men she is with may rape her.

In the resolution, the point where the story is concluded in some way, the expected tense is the preterite (Text 3-A, lines 40–41). The preterite is the most common tense in 83% of the resolution clauses of the Group 1 narratives. In the Group 2 data, 50% of the resolution clauses are in the preterite and 50% are in the present. In the Group 3 data, most of the resolution clauses, 50%, are in the present, followed with 32% of the clauses in the preterite. Sixteen percent of the clauses of the resolution for Group 3 are rendered in the past tense in English. Groups 2 and 3, bilingual and English-dominant speakers, then, are most similar in their use of the historical present as a device to give closure to the narrative. For Group 3 the use of English also serves as a device for this purpose.

In the evaluation sections, all three groups prefer the preterite to other tenses. This is especially true for Group 1 and Group 2, for whom the preterite is used in the evaluations over 50% of the time. However, in the Group 3 data, the preterite is used in the evaluation sections 32% of the time; the second most common strategy employed by these speakers in the evaluation sections is the use of English (see Text 3-A, lines 19, 24–26, 34). In fact, this is the section of the narrative where English is used most for Group 3 speakers. In 30% of the evaluation clauses, code-switching is employed.

All of the narratives in my sample are rich in evaluative devices, although as discussed, the same strategies are not used with the same frequency in each group. Silva-Corvalán (1988) indicates that narratives of second and, notably, third, generation Mexican American speakers, are marked by the paucity of evaluative devices. She states that speakers at the lower end of the bilingual continuum could provide the bare details of the narrative (complicating actions) but often do not produce evaluation devices similar to those used by first-generation speakers. In the Puerto Rican narratives, it is true that the use of English as an evaluation technique increases significantly in the Group 3 narratives (see Text 3-A, lines 19, 24–26, 34). However, the speakers of this group still use all of the narrative strategies employed by the Spanish-dominant speakers. To evaluate the complicating action, for example, as we have seen, Group 3 is adept at using the historical present in the same manner as the other groups (see Text 3-A, lines 28–33).

Overall, the verb tenses employed in all three groups of stories are appropriate to the given narrative components. There are no cases where the verb usage would be considered inaccurate from a prescriptive grammatical perspective. All speakers, from the Spanish-dominant to the English-dominant, produce well-formed, structurally complete narratives. The most striking differences in the narratives of the three groups fall in two categories. First, the Group 1 data are distinguished by the frequent use of the historical present to recount the past. Although all three groups of narrators employ this strategy, accounting for the high use of the present tense in the complicating action of all three groups, it is most frequent in the Group 1 narratives. Second, the narratives of the English-dominant speakers are distinguished by the use of code-switching in all components of the narrative, especially in the evaluation sections of the narratives (code-switching is dealt with more extensively in chap. 4). Unlike previous studies, which focus on the Spanish narratives of bilingual and English-dominant U.S.-based Latinos, I find that even Puerto Rican speakers who are more comfortable speaking English can produce narratives that are as well developed structurally as those produced by speakers who are Spanish-dominant. The performance of oral narratives is an activity that all community members can and do engage in successfully.

THE VERB SYSTEM—MOOD SELECTION

The majority of studies investigating the verb structure of U.S. Spanish concentrate on Mexican American Spanish; many studies (Gutiérrez, 1990; Lavandera, 1981; Silva-Corvalán, 1988, 1990) argue that the verb system of second- and third-generation Mexican Americans is considerably simplified compared to the first-generation verbal system. Early research on Latino verb usage can be criticized on methodological grounds. Many studies relied on artificial tests, such as grammaticality judgement exercises, which do not capture how people actually use language. The advantage of studying the verb structure through the expression of oral narratives is that all speakers are producing the same type of speech, a story about the past, thus allowing for a more valid and uniform basis of comparison. Admittedly, the downside is that the occurrence of less common verb forms is considerably reduced in the performance of narratives of past events.

Subjunctive usage is often cited as an area where simplification is underway in the Spanish spoken by U.S. Latinos (Escamilla, 1982; Floyd, 1978; Gutiérrez, 1990; Silva-Corvalán, 1988; Solé, 1977). Given the prevalence of this finding in other studies of U.S. Latino communities and its use to argue the loss of Spanish in minority language contexts, I investigate here subjunctive use in the Brentwood Puerto Rican community. To study mood selection in my sample, I considered the use of the subjunctive in 60 narratives. I analyzed categorical and variable use of the subjunctive in 20 narratives from each generational group.[1] Categorical uses of the subjunctive are those usages that are prescribed by Spanish grammar. For example, a Group 3 speaker in the narrative quoted earlier (Text 3-A) states:

1)   *"dehpuéh vino un moreno y dijo,* suéltenla" ["then a Black guy came and said, (you all) *let her go"*].

The use of the subjunctive verb form *suéltenla* is prescribed in this sentence because the quoted speaker is expressing a command in the plural; in Spanish, the subjunctive is categorically required in this context.

In another Group 3 narrative a speaker states:

2)   *"cuando* termine *con la lata te la doy"* ["when I *finish* with the can I'll give it to you"].

The use of the subjunctive verb is variable in the case of temporal clauses. In example 2, the subjunctive is used because a future action is referred to. On the other hand, in the sentence:

3)   *"nunca estudiaba cuando* salía *de la escuela"* ["I never studied when I *got out* of school"].

the verb in the temporal clause *salía* is expressed in the indicative mood because a past action is referred to. Therefore, there are some contexts where, according to prescriptive grammar, the subjunctive should al-

---

[1]The following analyses in chapters 3 and 4 are based on 20 narratives from each group for a total of 60 narratives. I needed to increase the sample size because of the relative infrequency of the verbs and other features I study.

ways be used and other cases where, depending on the context and semantic factors, its use is variable. Additionally, in some varieties of Spanish, such as the Puerto Rican variety, the use of the subjunctive is variable in some contexts where, according to prescriptive grammar, its use should be categorical. This is the case, for example, with expressions of emotional reaction such as: *me alegro de que* [I am happy that] and *me sorprende que* [it surprises me that]. In the following example from a Group 2 narrative, the verb in the comment clause is in the indicative; it could also have been produced in the subjunctive form *venga*:

4)   *"me alegro de que él* viene" ["I am glad that he *is coming."*].

My analysis reveals that, except for one type of grammatical construction (i.e., conditional sentences), there is little difference in mood selection across my three groups. Spanish-dominant, bilingual, and English-dominant speakers manipulate mood selection in similar ways, although the English-dominant speakers show slightly more variation.

To compare subjunctive use across groups in my sample, I considered the use of the subjunctive in 60 narratives. In studies such as these, it is important to calculate the overall use of indicative and subjunctive tenses, in order to get a general picture of verb frequencies. In a study of mood selection in the New York Puerto Rican community, Torres (1988) finds that the subjunctive represents 4.6% of total verb usage for first generation speakers and 4.1% of the total verb output for second generation. These totals come from 2-hour interviews with 10 speakers.

In this study, subjunctive use accounts for 3.4% of the total verb output in the narratives. The difference in frequency between this study and Torres (1988) is probably due to the specific speech type considered here. Oral narratives of past experience, which were culled from interview data for the purpose of this analysis, are not a speech type that lends itself to a high frequency of subjunctive usage; more frequent verb tenses, as we saw in the last section, are the indicative tenses, particularly the present, imperfect, and preterite indicative tenses.

What is important here is the comparison across the groups. No pattern of declining subjunctive use across generations emerges from the results. Instead, subjunctive use rises in the Group 2 data and then falls in the Group 3 data, but the frequency of use is still higher than that of the Group 1 data. Three percent of the verbs in the Group 1 data are subjunctive; 3.7% of the Group 2 verbs are subjunctive, as well as 3.4% of the Group 3 verbs.

Although overall production of subjunctive verbs does not differ very much across groups, it is important to analyze specific uses of the subjunctive. Few studies of subjunctive usage in U.S. Latino Spanish distinguish between variable and categorical mood selection or use data from actual speech production. For this analysis (following Ocampo,

1990), I first enumerated subjunctive use in the narratives according to traditional categories and then noted the presence or absence of subjunctive use in both categorical and variable linguistic contexts.[2]

The following table summarizes the results of this analysis according to presence or absence of the subjunctive in cases where its use is variable and in those contexts where, according to prescriptive grammar, the subjunctive should always be used.

Table 3.1 makes it clear that the rates of subjunctive use and even the contexts where mood choice is variable or obligatory are not very numerous. Again, this is due to the fact that subjunctive usage is not as frequent as indicative usage in narratives of past experience.

Figure 3.1 compares variable and categorical frequencies of subjunctive usage for the three groups of speakers. I considered all the contexts in the narratives where use of the subjunctive is variable, that is, those places where, according to prescriptive grammar, either a subjunctive or indicative verb form would be allowed. It is clear from this chart that

TABLE 3.1
Total Subjunctive Usage for the Three Groups

	Presence		*Absence*	
	Variable	*Categorical*	*Variable*	*Categorical*
Group 1	11	16	6	0
Group 2	9	17	6	0
Group 3	10	24	6	2

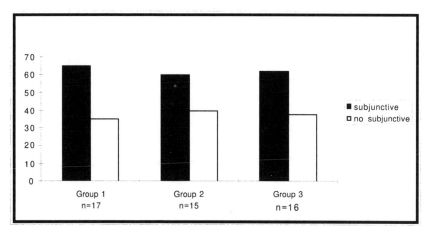

FIG. 3.1.   Mood choice in variable contexts: Percentage of variable contexts in which subjunctive is used.

[2]The following types of clauses were considered: comment, volitive, doubt, impossible, temporal, final, conditional, concessive, causative, negative causal, locative, and modal.

TABLE 3.2
Subjunctive Tenses Across Groups as Percentage

Subjunctive Type	Group 1	Group 2	Group 3
Present	33% (9)	69% (18)	62% (21)
Imperfect	48% (13)	31% (8)	20% (7)
Pluperfect	19% (5)	0% (0)	18% (6)

no significant difference obtains in the use of the subjunctive in variable contexts. In these cases, where mood choice is variable, all three groups use the subjunctive between 60% and 65% of the time, and they use the indicative 35% to 40% of the time.

With regard to categorical use, in all of the narratives there are only two cases where the subjunctive is not used in contexts where grammar rules would prescribe it. These two instances occur in the data of Group 3 (see Table 3.1).

I also calculated the frequencies of the various subjunctive tenses to see whether there were differences between the groups. Table 3.2 details the percentage of types of subjunctive appearing in the narratives.

Table 3.2 shows that in the Group 2 and Group 3 data, the present subjunctive is by far the most frequent tense. This is not true for Group 1, however, as the imperfect subjunctive occurs more often. Although Group 2 does not use any pluperfect subjunctive verbs forms in the narratives, these do appear in the data of Group 3, in almost exactly the same proportion as in the Group 1 data. Thus, whereas the imperfect subjunctive is used less frequently with each successive group, the overall picture does not suggest a gradual situation of subjunctive loss across groups.[3]

Most instances of imperfect subjunctive and pluperfect subjunctive usage occur in conditional sentences. Much variation has been found with regard to conditional sentences in many varieties of Spanish (cf. Lavandera 1984; Silva-Corvalán, 1984). According to prescriptive grammar, both the protasis (a subordinate clause expressing a condition in a conditional sentence) and the apodosis (the conclusion of a conditional

[3]Ocampo (1990) analyzes the use of the subjective in the speech of Mexican Americans from three generations and concludes that the subjunctive is used considerably less with each succeeding generational group. The third generation uses the subjunctive less in contexts where the subjunctive is categorically required. Significantly, Ocampo finds that the subjunctive appears considerably less frequently among third-generation speakers in contexts where its use is variable. In this latter case, the subjunctive is used only 22% of the time, compared to 60% of the time for second-generation speakers, and 79% of the time for first generation-speakers. Although Ocampo studies a Spanish-speaking community in a language contact situation, the differences in my findings suggest that each community is unique and tendencies found in one Spanish-speaking community in the United States should not be generalized to others.

sentence) should be in the indicative in if-clauses when the speaker believes that the condition will be fulfilled. If the condition is improbable or denied, usually the verb of the protasis is in the imperfect subjunctive (IS), for events in the present or future, or the pluperfect subjunctive (PP), for events in the past, and the result is in the conditional (Solé & Solé, 1977). In the Group 1 data, all if clauses are expressed in the subjunctive. The conditional is never used, not even in cases where the protasis is contrary to fact; rather a subjunctive form is used, as in examples 5 and 6 produced by Group 1 speakers:

5)   *"Si yo hubiera sabido* (PP), *hubiera cogido* (PP) *el día completo libre."* ["If I would have known, I would have taken the whole day off."]

6)   *"Si yo la hubiera tenido (PP) [la ayuda], yo no hubiera tenido (PP) la experiencia que yo estuve."* [4] ["If I had had it, I wouldn't have had the experience I had."]

In the Group 2 data, conditional sentences do not appear in the narratives. In the Group 3 data, more patterns of conditional sentences obtain. The Group 1 pattern of pluperfect subjunctive in both clauses occurs here also, as in example 7. However, it is clear that if–then clauses present a special problem for Group 3 speakers. Examples 7 to 9 show other combinations that occur in Group 3 data.

7)   *"Si algo hubiera pasado* (PP) *no hubiera tenido* (pp) *prueba de ninguna clase."* ["If something would have happened I wouldn't have had any kind of proof."]

8)   *"Si yo no hubiera hecho* (PP) *eso no te sabría* (C) *decir donde estuviera* (IS) *yo."* ["If I hadn't had done that I wouldn't know what to tell you where I would be."]

9)   *"Si no fuera* (IS) *porque yo hubiera sabido* (PP) *que tú tenías quince años yo te hubiera mandao* (PP) *al hospital."* ["If it hadn't been because I had known that you are fifteen years old I would have sent you to the hospital."]

In example 8, produced by a Group 3 speaker, the protasis conforms to both standard and Group 1 usage, but the result clause is more complicated, as it consists of a complex clause. The first part of the result clause is expressed in the conditional, which is standard usage. However, the complement of *sabría decir*, according to prescriptive grammar, should also appear in the conditional, or following Group 1 usage in the

---

[4]This speaker consistently uses the preterite of *estar* (*estuve*) where the preterite of *tener* (*tuve*) would be the standard form. She is the only person in the sample to display this type of usage.

pluperfect subjunctive. Instead, an imperfect subjunctive form (*estuviera*) appears. In example 9, the protasis should be expressed in the pluperfect subjunctive because at this point in the narrative, the speaker is referring to a past event; also the clause: *porque yo hubiera sabido* would usually be expressed in the indicative because it represents something the speaker found out earlier according to the narrative. The result clause in this case is also expressed in the pluperfect subjunctive in accordance with Group 1 usage.

Because there were few examples of conditional structures, it is difficult to generalize from the foregoing data; but they can be identified as one context where there is much variation in the speech of Group 3. However, it is worth noting that Group 1 examples of conditional constructions do not concur with standard usage. According to these data, as well as other studies, mood and tense choice appear to be in flux with regard to these structures. We can conclude that, except for these variable conditional clauses, the subjunctive appears infrequently in all narratives of past events for the three generational groups.

In conclusion, when the subjunctive mood does appear, it is used similarly by all three groups, except in conditional constructions, where there is more variation in the Group 3 data. Although this is the only case in my data where mood and tense show more variation for Group 3 than for Groups 1 and 2, it is important to remember that mood is not always predictable in many situations and this is the case even in Spanish varieties not in contact with English. For example, Blake (1985) reports that for his middle-class Mexico City informants, variation occurs with matrices of doubt and attitude. He argues that mood choice may be more determined by pragmatic factors (such as shared information or a speaker's emotive state) than by any categorical rule. In this study, traditional use of the subjunctive occurs in the majority of all cases. These results indicate that mood selection across the three groups is similar. Even speakers who are English-dominant adhere to community norms of subjunctive usage. Although the subjunctive occurs in less than 5% of all speech, the Brentwood Puerto Rican bilingual and English-dominant speakers apparently have enough Spanish input and sufficient practice in the language to incorporate this feature in their oral narratives and to do so in relatively comparable ways.

OTHER POSSIBLE LINGUISTIC SITES
OF VERB SIMPLIFICATION

Similar findings are noted when other potential occasions of verb simplification are analyzed in the Brentwood Puerto Rican data. In the production of oral narratives, bilingual and English-dominant speakers manipulate the verb structures with as much dexterity as Spanish-dominant speakers. As we have seen, analysis of the Spanish of other bilingual and English-dominant Latinos in the United States suggests that simplification of the verb structures is indeed underway; however, the Spanish of the Brentwood Puerto Rican community, although sharing the condition of being the minority language in an English-dominant context, does not seem to show the same tendencies. In this section, I document that Brentwood bilingual and English-dominant Puerto Ricans maintain verbal integrity and complexity in contexts other than subjunctive usage. This analysis includes a comparison with data from the Los Angeles Mexican American community.

Silva-Corvalán (1990) identifies several processes of simplification and loss of certain verb forms and functions in her Los Angeles Mexican database. These findings are relevant to the Brentwood Puerto Rican Spanish situation because the two communities share a similar Spanish–English language contact situation and the analyses also place speakers along a bilingual continuum. Silva-Corvalán suggests that a series of changes is occurring with periphrastic constructions (formed by the use of auxilary verbs) in Mexican American Spanish affecting the verbs *ser* [to be], *estar* [to be], and *ir* [to go]. She notices the following three characteristics in the speech samples of second and third generation bilinguals: a) most use the preterite *fue* [were/was] exclusively with the meaning of *went*; b) they tend to use the imperfect forms of *ser* and *estar* [*era* and *estaba*] in both perfective and imperfective contexts; and c) the verb *ir* [to go] loses its lexical meaning and is used by these speakers mostly as an auxiliary in the periphrastic phrase: *ir + a + infinitive* [to be going to + infinitive]. She asserts that the lexical and paradigmatic gap created by the loss of the lexical form *iba* [past imperfect form of to go] is filled by the use of periphrastic constructions such as *estaba + -ando* [was + progressive form].

These results suggest that the verb system of Mexican Americans is being reduced and simplified. I accepted these three findings in the Mexican American data as hypotheses to be explored in the Brentwood narratives under review here.

A sign that a change in the direction suggested by Silva-Corvalán is underway in the Brentwood data can be detected in terms of the uses for *fue*. Silva-Corvalán states that second- and third-generation speakers use *fue* [was] exclusively to convey the meaning *went*. I do not find this to be the case in all my data, although for Group 3, this usage is the most common. Fifty-four percent of the time (84 of 155 respondents), *fue* functions with the meaning *went* in Group 3 narratives, as example 10 illustrates:

10) *"El aprendió rápido y* fue *pa la escuela en septiembre."* ["He learned very quickly and he *went* to school in September."]

In the other 46% of the time, *fue* is used with the meaning *was*, as in example 11:

11)   *"En Coram* fue *el único sitio que tuve problemah por acá."*
        ["Coram *was* the only place where I had problems over here."]

In contrast, *fue* is used with the meaning *went* 35% of the time (46 of 132 respondents) for Group 2, and 28% (28 of 105 respondents) for Group 1. Whereas these results do not suggest that *fue* is currently reduced to one semantic meaning, they do indicate that Group 3 favors one meaning over the other. The data perhaps also suggest a tendency toward reduction of the type found in the Mexican American data where Silva-Corvalán finds a one-to-one correspondence between form and meaning.

In the Brentwood data, unlike the Mexican American data, there is no case where *estaba* (imperfect form of the verb *estar*) is used instead of *fue* (preterite form of the verb *ser*), but in three cases *era* (imperfect form of the verb *ser*) is used instead of a preterite in Group 3 narratives. In one example the verb should have been rendered in the preterite *fue* [was] because this utterance comes at the end of a narrative:

12)   *"Esa experience no* era *tan buena."* ["That experience *wasn't* so good."]

The three cases constitute less than 1% of the time when either *era* or *estaba* is used in perfective contexts. This never occurs in the Group 1 or Group 2 narratives. In the Brentwood data, therefore, the tendency for confusion and reduction of forms does not occur with regard to *fue*.

With the use of *iba + a + infinitive* [was going to + infinitive] a pattern quite different from the Mexican American data emerges. Compared to the Brentwood Spanish-dominant and bilingual groups, the English-dominant group uses *iba* with its lexical meaning (example 13) more frequently than in periphrastic constructions (example 14).

13)   *"Mi mamá sufrió mucho por mi, yo hice muchah cosah mala y me* iba *por la semana botá en la cuidad."* ["My mother suffered a lot because of me, I did a lot of bad things and *would go* for a week hangin' out in the city"]
14)   *"Yo no pensaba que él* iba a hacer *una cosa así."* ["I didn't think he *was going to* do something like that."]

Iba is used in periphrastic constructions 31% of the time (19 of 62 respondents) in the Group 3 data, 58% of the time (22 of 38 respondents) in the Group 2 data, and 48% of the time (15 of 31 respondents) in the

Group 1 data. This means that in 69% of the cases where *iba* is used in Group 3 data, it retains its lexical meaning. *Iba* is used with its lexical meaning more frequently in the Group 3 data than in the Group 2 and Group 1 data. It held its lexical meaning in 42% of its appearances in the Group 2 data, and approximately half the time it appears as such in Group 1 data. These frequencies do not suggest that *iba* is losing its lexical meaning and is now serving more as a grammatical form, as has been suggested could be the case in the Mexican American data where second and third generation speakers use *iba* mostly in periphrastic constructions.

Therefore, in terms of the three hypotheses suggested by the Mexican American data, for Brentwood, a mixed picture emerges. There does appear to be a tendency toward a decrease in the range of functions of the verb *fue* with each successive generation. Also, there is only a slight use of *ser* in the imperfect in a perfective context. Both these cases represent low frequency phenomena, especially when compared to the Mexican American situation. Finally, and surprisingly, the Puerto Rican Spanish-dominant group uses *ir* in periphrastic constructions much more frequently than the other two groups, which is exactly the opposite result as in the Mexican American context.

Thus, the type of interrelated cases of simplification that obtains in the Los Angeles Spanish speaking community is not evident in the narratives of the Puerto Rican community I studied. This suggests that, whereas the Mexican American and Puerto Rican communities share many characteristics, the language use and language loss patterns present in one community do not necessarily occur at the same rate, or even in the same direction as in the other community.

Summarizing the findings concerning the verb system used in the oral narratives, I conclude that simplification of the type documented in the studies of Mexican American speech is generally not evidenced in the narratives across the bilingual continuum of Brentwood Puerto Rican speakers. Although there are several areas (for example, uses of the verb form *fue*, and variation in conditional constructions) where a case could be made for the early stages of simplification, overall, the verb system is as rich for Group 3 speakers, as it is for Group 1 and Group 2 speakers. Also, as we have seen, verb usage corresponds to the different components of the narrative structure used by all three groups of speakers. A possible explanation for why the results differ from Silva-Corvalán's (1990) could be found in terms of the data collected. I restricted my analysis to language use in oral narratives, whereas this is not the case in other studies that gather speech samples from interviews and conversations. The advantage of restricting myself to one speech type is that it results in a much more controlled and reliable data base than is possible in other studies.

Linguistic attrition is thus not confirmed when we compare Puerto Rican English-dominant bilingual speech with the speech of Spanish-dominant and more balanced bilinguals in Brentwood. These findings further suggest that different varieties of Spanish in the United States evolve in their own manner and at their own rates, and that generalizations across all U.S. Spanish varieties are unwarranted.

NARRATIVE CLAUSE STRUCTURE

The verb system is not the only site of change noted in the literature on U.S. Spanish; studies (Gutiérrez, 1990; Silva Corvalán, 1988) also suggest that U.S. Spanish undergoes simplification at the level of clause structure. Many researchers (Beaman, 1984; Bernstein, 1970; Hill, 1973; Kalman 1985) posit that complexity in syntax can be measured in terms of the type, number and depth of embedding of subordinate clauses in discourse.[5] In this section I analyze syntactic complexity as measured by the use of subordination in the narratives of the three groups of Puerto Ricans. I argue that the oral narratives produced by bilingual and English-dominant speakers are as complex in terms of clause structure as the oral narratives of Spanish-dominant community members.

Manual Gutiérrez (1990), in a study of the maintenance of subordinate clauses across three generations of Mexican American speakers, argues that as dominance in Spanish decreases, the frequency of use of subordination decreases, from 43% in the first group, to 29% in the second group, and 23% in the third group; the type of subordination used also differs across the three groups.

---

[5]Salah (1990) suggests that subordinate clause complexity, specifically the embedding depth of clauses, can be used as a measure of competence in a language. She finds that more advanced learners of a second language show greater clause complexity in their language when compared to beginning students. Another piece of evidence that supports the idea that sentences with subordinate constructions are more complex is the fact that such sentences take a longer time to process then do simple sentences (see also Beaman, 1984; Bernstein, 1970; Hill, 1973; Knoll, 1977; Lope Blanch, 1983, 1990).

Whereas much linguistic and educational literature equates degree of subordination with greater syntactic complexity, some authors have pointed out that the relationship is not that transparent. Thompson (1987) argues, for example, that the term *subordination* is ambiguous because it is used to refer to elements that are very different and have a wide range of functions. Knoll (1977) develops the idea that what is grammatically considered as subordinate, might in fact convey the most important information in the utterance. Schleppegrell (1991) shows how it can be misleading to categorize clauses according to the subordinating conjunctions that introduce clauses, because these can sometimes function as coordinating conjunctions or interactional markers. Romaine (1984) questions the equation usually made between degree of subordination and cognitive development. She stresses how important it is to consider the specific contexts of speech, because syntactic complexity can be produced differently according to context.

Given the view on subordination represented in the majority of the studies reviewed, I consider here the following hypothesis: As dominance in Spanish decreases, syntactic complexity in the narratives, as evidenced by the use of subordinate structures, also decreases. To test this hypothesis, I calculated the frequency of occurrence of three types of strategies for the connecting clauses of the Puerto Rican oral narratives: implicit sequencing, coordination, or subordination. The following portion of a Group 2 narrative (Text 3-C) contains all three types of connectors:

> Text 3-C
> 1) *Mi hermano me vino*
> 2) *y me dijo el problema*
> 3) *que el tenía*
> 4) *yo llamé enseguida a* human rights
> 5) *y le dije*
> 6) *pasa esto y esto y esto*
> 7) and I don't think that's right
> 8) *la policia quiere*
> 9) *que lo respete*
> 10) *ellos tienen*
> 11) *que darse a respetar*
> 12) *para que loh respeten*
> 13) *ellos tienen que respetar a los puertorriqueñoh también*
>
> [1) my brother came to me
> 2) and told me the problem
> 3) that he had
> 4) right away I called human rights
> 5) and I told them
> 6) this is happening and this and this
> 7) and I don't think that's right
> 8) the police wants
> 9) you to respect them
> 10) they have to
> 11) act in a way to make themselves respected
> 12) so that others will respect them
> 13) they have to respect the Puerto Ricans also]

A clause consists of a unit that has at least a verb as its nucleus. It may stand alone or include other elements such as subjects, objects, and adverbials. Implicit sequencing refers to those cases in the narratives where no coordinating or subordinating conjunctions are used to link clauses; rather, the speaker relies on the context or other means to provide continuity, for example, lines 4, 8, 10, 13. Coordination entails the joining of two independent clauses by means of coordinating conjunctions; these can be copulative (*y, ni* [and, neither]), distributive (*estos . . . aquellos, tan pronto* [these . . . those, as soon as]), disjunctive (*o* [or]), or adversative (*pero, sino* [but, rather]), for example lines 2, 5, 7 (line 7 is an example of a clause produced in English in a Spanish language narrative). Subordination consists of the joining of an independent clause with one or more dependent clauses. Each subordinate clause has a finite verb and is usually introduced by a subordinating conjunction (*que, quien* [that, who], e.g., lines, 3, 6, 9, 11, 12). Subordinate clauses always have one of the following syntactic functions: subject, subject complement, adjective, adjectival complement, verb complement, adverbial phrase, and direct or indirect complement of another complement (Gili Gaya, 1968).

Table 3.3 presents the frequencies and percentages for each type of Spanish clause sequencing in the 60 narratives of the three groups. Also included in the table is the frequency of English clauses for each group.

In terms of Spanish connectors, a similar pattern obtains across the three groups of narratives (the use of English in the narratives is discussed in chap. 4). The most frequent means of connecting narrative clauses for all groups is implicit sequencing with no explicit marking by any connective at all. This is not unusual, because narratives have structural characteristics that render them easy to follow. For example, all narratives have a beginning, middle, and end, and they usually contain a series of details that are temporally ordered. Coordination and subordination, on the other hand, combine different elements of the story in specific ways. When we compare coordination and subordination, we see that the rest of the sequencing of clauses is almost evenly divided between these two types in all three groups. Groups 2 and 3 use subordination slightly more than Group 1, but the difference appears minor.

All groups prefer the two least complex types of connectives, implicit sequencing and coordinating conjunctions, over subordinate conjunctions; the former account for more than 50% of the connectives in all cases. Given my hypothesis, that subordination will decrease with

TABLE 3.3
Clause Linking Devices in the Narratives

	Group 1		Group 2		Group 3	
Implicit	37.5%	(336)	39.2%	(269)	31.5%	(307)
Coordination	31.2%	(279)	26.0%	(179)	26.0%	(255)
Subordination	27.4%	(245)	28.7%	(197)	28.1%	(274)
English Clauses	3.8%	(34)	5.9%	(41)	14.2%	(139)
Group Clause Total		894		686		975

increasing English dominance, the most surprising result is the lack of difference between the three groups, especially as concerns overall frequency of subordination in the narratives. As seen in Table 3.3, the three groups are very similar. For Group 1, 27.4% of their clauses are connected through subordinate clauses, while this is true for 28.7% of the clauses in the Group 2 data, and 28.1% in the Group 3 data.

In order to investigate whether different preferences for subordination linking strategies across the three groups exist, I classified the subordinate clauses according to their grammatical function within the sentence, as nominal clauses, adjectival clauses, and adverbial clauses. The following examples from Group 2 narratives are complex sentences with the subordinate clause emphasized.

15) nominal clause: "*Al terminarse el año supimos* que la nena tenía un problema en oír." ["At the end of the year we found out *that the girl had a hearing problem.*"]

16) adjectival clause: "*En Headstart uno de los servicios* que le ofrecen a los niños *es el* hearing screening." ["In Headstart one of the services *that they offer the children* is the hearing screening."]

17) adverbial clause: "*Yo hablé con él* cuando eso pasó" ["I talked with him *when that happened.*"]

Floyd (1990) reviews studies that attempt to determine the order of acquisition for different types of subordinate clauses in Spanish by monolingual and bilingual children. Although the results are inconclusive, most studies suggest that nominal and adverbial clauses are acquired earlier than adjectival clauses. Thus, we might argue that these are less complex than adjectival subordination, and following my initial hypothesis, we would expect that the Spanish-dominant speakers would have a higher frequency of adjectival clauses. However, again, this does not occur.

The data presented in Table 3.4 indicate that, contrary to our hypothesis, all groups follow a similar pattern. For all groups, nominal and adverbial clauses are more frequent than adjectival clauses. The adverbial clause is the most common type of subordination used by Groups 2 and 3; the nominal clause is the most frequent for Group 1; but adverbial clauses are almost as common. The frequency indices for Groups 2 and 3 are almost identical to each other. The greatest variation among the three groups occurs with Group 1, which has at least 7% more nominal clauses and 8% fewer adverbial clauses than the other two groups. Group 3 does have the least frequent number of adjectival clauses, presumed to be the most complex type of clause, but the difference across all three groups with respect to this type of clause seems minimal.

TABLE 3.4
Frequency of Three Subordinate Clauses Types

	Group 1		Group 2		Group 3	
Nominal	43.6%	(107)	36.0%	(71)	35.4%	(97)
Adjectival	15.0%	(37)	14.2%	(28)	13.8%	(38)
Adverbial	41.2%	(101)	49.7%	(98)	50.7%	(139)
Group Total		245		197		274

The nominal clauses can function as a subject, direct object, or indirect object. For all groups, the vast majority of the noun clauses function as direct objects as in example 15. Because direct and indirect speech are very common in oral narrative performance, it is revealing to look at this specific use of the noun clause and to investigate whether the three groups rely on these strategies differently.

In the narratives, when speakers present the speech that others utter they can directly quote the talk (direct speech) or they can present it without a direct quote using various grammatical distancing strategies (indirect speech). For instance, example 18 is an example of direct speech, whereas 19 is rendered in indirect style.

18) *"me dice: ay, no te pongas altera"* ["she tells me, oh don't get excited"]
19) *"la maestra decía que no entendía porque la nena había estado diez meses con ella"* ["the teacher said that she didn't understand why the girl had been with her ten months"]

When narrators use direct speech, they are purportedly reproducing what occurred in the original event being recounted. Quoted speech powerfully reinforces the narrative because it adds coherence to the relationship between the narrator and the past experience (Pellicer, 1992). Recreated direct speech renders the narrative more lively and is considered a sophisticated internal evaluation device. Silva-Corvalán (1988), for example, claims that speakers who are less proficient in Spanish do not tend to use reported direct speech in their narratives, to the extent that more proficient speakers do. On the other hand, indirect speech, by its nature entails a distancing from the actual stated proposition. This means that at the grammatical level, paraphrasing speech also involves the use of complex syntax and morphology, again usually expected of Spanish-dominant speakers.

This apparent contradiction has led two researchers studying the Mexican American community to come to the same conclusion, namely that bilinguals suffer simplification of speech, regardless of whether speakers use direct speech frequently or infrequently. Gutiérrez (1990), in his study of oral narratives, states that with each succeeding Mexican American generational group the frequency of indirect speech diminishes, whereas frequency of direct speech increases. He notes that indirect speech often involves the use of more complicated verb morphology and syntax in the subordinate clause, and speculates that the second and especially the third generation might use direct speech as a strategy to circumvent more complex indirect speech construction. This is a finding contradictory to that of the study by Silva-Corvalán (1988), in which less proficient speakers are said not to use direct speech to the degree that more proficient speakers do. Silva-Corvalán's conclusion is that the low frequency of direct speech is evidence of a failure of less proficient Spanish speakers to perform narratives as well as Spanish-dominant speakers. It is ironic that in these two studies of the same community, both frequent *and* infrequent use of direct speech in narrative performance are used as evidence of simplification of Mexican American Spanish. Apparently these speakers are in a no-win situation! Whatever they do is viewed as simplification.

Given this confusing background in the existing literature, I examined the cases in which the nominal clauses function as direct objects, specifically the cases of direct and indirect speech in the narratives. I focused on the constructions following verbs of saying (i.e., *decir, contar, gritar*, and so on [to say, to tell, to scream]); in other words, examples like 18 and 19 taken from Group 2. The results from my research (Table 3.5) do not suggest a progression of reduced simplification.

Group 1 renders 81% of the verbs of saying in direct style and 19% in indirect style. Sixty-nine percent of the verbs of saying are in direct style, whereas 31% are in indirect style in the Group 2 data. For Group 3, 86% of the verbs are in direct style, whereas 14% are in indirect style. Although Group 3 does have the lowest frequency of indirect speech style, there is not a progressive loss of indirect speech style across groups. There is a significant increase in indirect speech and consequently a decrease in direct style in Group 2 narratives. Group 3 narrators are slightly more likely than Group 1 speakers to use direct speech as an internal evaluation device (See Text 3-A, lines 21, 25, 34, 36, 37) and more likely to use this type of evaluation than are Group 2 speakers. Therefore, use of neither direct speech nor indirect speech in the narratives supports claims of simplification.

TABLE 3.5
Direct Style Versus Indirect Style of Quoting

	Group 1		Group 2		Group 3	
Direct Style	81%	(55)	69%	(27)	86%	(60)
Indirect Style	19%	(13)	31%	(12)	14%	(10)
Group Total		68		39		70

TABLE 3.6
Frequency of Nine Adverbial Clause Types

	Group 1		Group 2		Group 3	
Temporal	33%	(33)	26%	(24)	28%	(39)
Modal	6%	(6)	5%	(5)	9%	(13)
Locative	3%	(3)	3%	(3)	3%	(4)
Comparative	3%	(3)	2%	(2)	1%	(2)
Consecutive	3%	(3)	4%	(4)	7%	(10)
Causal	36%	(36)	42%	(39)	24%	(34)
Final	2%	(2)	6%	(6)	4%	(6)
Conditional	15%	(15)	12%	(11)	20%	(28)
Concessive	0%	(0)	0%	(0)	3%	(4)
Group Total		101		94		140

Another test of possible simplification concerns adjectival clauses (relative clauses), which are acquired latest by children, and therefore are presumed to be the most complex type of subordination. Whereas in Gutiérrez' (1990) study, there is a progressive decline in the use of adjectival clauses across generations, in the Puerto Rican narratives they are used similarly by all groups. For Group 1, of all subordinate clauses, 15% are adjectival clauses; for Group 2, adjectival clauses account for 14.2% of the subordinate clause total; and for Group 3, 13.8%. For all groups, they are the least frequent clause type present in the narratives (see Table 3.4).

In contrast, adverbial clauses are frequently used in the narratives. This is not surprising, given that locating events in place, time, and space, and explaining how actions and happenings occur, is often accomplished through the use of adverbials. Adverbial clauses can be grouped according to their semantics. Table 3.6 presents the frequency of types of adverbial clauses represented in the data.

Temporal, causal, and conditional adverbial clauses account for more than 70% of the adverbial clauses in all three groups. Examples 20 through 22 illustrate each of these three types:

20) temporal clause: "cuando yo termine *te lo doy*" [*"when I finish I will give it to you"*];
21) causal clause: "*cogió la nena* para que pudiera seguir" ["she took the girl *so that she could continue"*];
22) conditional clause: "si los padres los llevan al doctor *el pediatrician les hace un examen*" [*"if the parents take them to the doctor* the pediatrician gives them an exam"].

For both Group 1 and Group 2, the most common adverbial clauses, in order of frequency, are: causal > temporal > conditional. For Group 3, although we find the same three most common adverbial clauses, the order of frequency is slightly different: temporal > causal > conditional.[6]

Reduction in the use of the various adverbial clause types may indicate simplification. In the Brentwood Puerto Rican data, each group produces a comparable range of adverbial types. In fact, whereas Groups 1 and 2 use eight different types of adverbials, Group 3 utilizes nine. Cocessive adverbials are present in the Group 3 data, whereas they do not appear in the data of the other two groups.

These results contrast with those of other studies. Gutiérrez (1990), finds that a greater range of types of adverbial clauses is present in the first generation data he collected on Mexican Americans. Lack of use of a range of adverbials, especially in the third generation, is taken to be yet another sign of simplification of Mexican American Spanish. This type of simplification is not apparent in the Brentwood Puerto Rican Spanish.

In all regards, I did not find a pattern of reduction of syntactic complexity in terms of a diminishing use of subordination across groups of Puerto Rican speakers, as Gutiérrez (1990) observes in the Mexican American data. The frequency of overall use of subordination does not decrease linearly across the three groups; in fact, group subordination totals are very similar. Also, in terms of nominal clauses, all three groups produce low frequencies of indirect speech. Group 2 produces almost twice as many instances (31%) of indirect speech as the other two groups. Group 3 does produce the least amount of indirect speech; only 14% of all their nominal clauses of saying are rendered indirectly. Finally, the range of adverbial clauses is comparable across all three groups, with Group 3 producing one more type than Groups 2 and 3.

CONCLUSION

A detailed analysis of verb use and clause structure in the narratives reveals that the most salient difference between the narratives of the three groups is the use of English in the narratives of Group 3. But in terms of the Spanish verb system and clause complexity, the narratives produced by all participants are strikingly similar.

Given the findings of other studies, the question remains as to why so little difference is found when comparing the grammatical system of narratives told by speakers who represent a range of Spanish proficiencies. Although Group 3 speakers are English-dominant and use Spanish in a limited range of contexts, narratives of personal experiences are a

---

[6]It is interesting to note that in Beaman's (1984) study of English language narratives, the most frequent adverbial structures are also the temporal, conditional, and causal clauses.

speech type that they are familiar with and use on those occasions when they speak Spanish with family and friends. Telling stories about things that have happened to them is probably the most common use of the Spanish language that English-dominant speakers engage in when speaking with Spanish monolingual or Spanish-dominant persons. Out of respect for their Spanish-dominant elder relatives and friends, the younger Brentwood community members make the effort involved in communicating in their weaker language. As one English-dominant young man notes, *"Con los mayores yo siempre trato de hablar español porque ellos lo entienden mejor"* ["with the older people I always try to speak Spanish because they understand it better"]. Even though young Puerto Ricans are using less Spanish than previous generations (chaps. 2 and 3), the fact that they can still produce such well-formed narratives serves as evidence that they are attempting to maintain community norms of language use.

It may also be, as Labov (1972) suggests, that narrative as a whole contrasts with ordinary conversation, which he claims has a much more complex structure. Telling narratives of personal experience in the research context constitutes a case of unplanned discourse, or discourse that is not organizationally prepared or previously thought out. According to Ochs (1979), one characteristic of this type of speech is that morphosyntactic structures acquired earlier in life predominate. These would tend to be the less complex structures.

Lope Blanch (1983) agrees with this perspective when he asserts that education is the most important variable in determining the more frequent usage of subordination in the narratives he studied. It is difficult to gauge the impact of education in the present study. Of the Group 1 speakers, the only group that was educated in the Spanish language in Puerto Rico, 2 had finished high school and the other 3 had not gone further than the sixth grade. None of the speakers in Groups 2 or 3 had studied Spanish formally in school. In terms of their educational levels in English, Group 3 speakers had, on the average, more overall education than Group 1 members. Most had completed high school and two Group 3 members had completed two years of college. Because the Group 3 members had levels of clause complexity similar to those of the other two groups, a question raised by this study is to what degree narration skills and the use of syntactic complexity in one language is transferable to another.

Whatever the role of education may be, the fact remains that, regardless of Spanish proficiency, when all three groups of speakers produce oral narratives, they use similar verb systems and clause structures. Linguistic attrition is not apparent in the performance of oral narrative in Spanish by English-dominant bilinguals. Because one difference that does obtain is the greater use of English in this group's narratives, code-mixing is taken up in the next chapter.

Code-Mixing and Lexical Innovations as Narrative Strategies

4

INTRODUCTION

As seen in chapters 1 and 2, the Puerto Rican community of Brentwood avails itself of a diverse range of codes. Speakers are not equally comfortable employing all codes, although they usually have a passive knowledge of most of them (Elías-Olivares, 1982; Pedraza, 1987; Torres, 1989). Along the "bilingualism continuum" (Kachru, 1985), in Brentwood, as in many Hispanic communities, one finds speakers who are dominant in Spanish, others who have different degrees of proficiency in Spanish and English, or are balanced bilinguals, as well as some who are English-dominant. Despite the prevalence of speakers who manipulate multiple codes, there is a lack of research about the "bilingual's creativity" (Kachru, 1985, 1986), or the strategies used by speakers in these communities with resources from more than one language.

One of the main areas of interest in the study of Spanish in the United States is the influence of English on Spanish language varieties. The focus is usually on how English, the dominant language, negatively impacts on Spanish, both structurally and in terms of overall language maintenance. However, studies rarely discuss the bilingual's creativity in the use of two languages. Setting up the discussion in terms of negative impact precludes consideration of how English and Spanish are used in creative and innovative ways in the repertoire of the bilingual. The latter is the focus of the present chapter. I study the discourse functions of English language borrowing and code-mixing in Spanish language narratives of Brentwood speakers across the cline of bilingualism (Kachru, 1985). I also analyze the narratives produced by Spanish-dominant, bilingual, and English-dominant speakers to determine how they incorporate English into their Spanish language production. Finally, I examine the borrowing patterns and code-mixing[1]

---

[1]The use of the terminology on code-mixing and code-switching varies among investigators. For example, Appel and Muysken (1987) use the terms interchangeably, whereas Hamers and Banc (1990) use the terms to refer to different processes. I refer to code-mixing in the sense used by Kachru (1983): "code-mixing entails transferring linguistic units from one code to another. Such a transfer (mixing) results in a new restricted or not so restricted code of linguistic interaction" (p. 194). In code-switching, the alternation of one language to the other usually corresponds with a change of participant, social situation, and so on (cf. Blom & Gumperz, 1972; Sridhar, 1978).

strategies employed by the three groups of speakers and demonstrate that some are community-wide, whereas others are specific to a group with a particular proficiency in Spanish or English. This analysis of the oral narratives reveals that Brentwood Puerto Ricans, especially bilingual and English-dominant speakers, use the languages at their disposal in innovative and creative ways.

BORROWING

All languages incorporate borrowed items from other languages. When two languages coexist in one environment the likelihood for borrowing increases. Although this phenomenon can be bidirectional, usually the less dominant language incorporates more items than the dominant language. Compared to varieties of Spanish not in contact with English, U.S. Spanish varieties obviously contain more English language items. Given that vocabulary is one of the most noticeable parts of the language, the borrowings into U.S. Spanish give these varieties the appearance of being heavily influenced by English. In this section, I consider the frequency, as well as the type of borrowings that occur in the three groups of narratives. The analysis leads to the conclusion that Brentwood Puerto Rican speakers, especially bilingual and English-dominant speakers, creatively integrate English in their Spanish language oral narratives at the single word level.

I distinguish among four types of borrowings in Puerto Rican Spanish: loanwords, merged calques, independent calques, and phrasal calques.[2] I define these terms and give examples of each below. In my analysis I consider all single-word English utterances as potential loanwords.[3] I further divide loanwords into two types: items from English in the Spanish discourse that are borrowed, and phonologically and morphologically integrated into Spanish (as in example 1), and

---

[2]In this section, I am following the useful taxonomy of borrowing phenomena presented in Otheguy and Garcia's (1988) study.

[3]It is difficult to distinguish borrowing from code-mixing at the single word level. An English word in Spanish discourse may be a code-mix, an idiosyncratic use limited to one speaker on one occasion (nonce borrowing), or a bona fide loanword used by many community members. These different phenomena entail different linguistic processes and are probably signifiers of differing bilingual ability. Poplack and Sankoff (1984) propose a set of linguistic and social criteria that, taken together, are good indicators of loanword status. These are frequency of use, native language displacement, morphophonemic and syntactic integration, and community acceptability. As more of these criteria are met, we can be more confident that we are dealing with loanword adoption rather that another phenomenon. As Poplack and Sankoff (1984) demonstrate, a complex procedure would be necessary for this type of analysis. Given the nature of my data, I cannot determine conclusively whether single English words in the Spanish narratives are code-switches, loanwords, or nonce borrowings; thus, I follow the practive of linguists such as Poplack, Sankoff, and Miller (1988) of considering all single-word English utterances as potential loanwords.

items that are not integrated into Spanish at the word level (example 2):

1)   *"Yo* quitié *ese trabajo."* ["I *quit* that job."]
2)   *"El* van *de los exámenes vino tarde."* ["The *van* for the tests arrived late."]

Calques are items that already exist in the borrowing language but that acquire a new meaning from the lending language. In the following example:

3)   *"Voy a llenar una* aplicación *para un trabajo."* ["I am going to complete an *application* for a job."],

the word *aplicación* exists in Spanish with the meaning "to apply or to attribute," but is used in a new manner, its meaning calqued from the English word *application.* In a Spanish variety uninfluenced by English, the term would be *solicitud.*

Phonologically merged calques are one-word items that resemble English either phonologically or by being related in meaning in some way. For example, *registrar* and *register* are phonologically very close and the meanings are similar. In varieties uninfluenced by English the Spanish word *registrar* means to inspect, examine, or to search. In varieties influenced by English, it is used to mean "to sign up for," *to register*, as in the following example from a Group 3 narrative:

4)   *"Yo voy a seguir con la escuela, en septiembre me voy a* registrar *en el* community college." ["I am going to continue with school, in September I am going to *register* at the community college."]

Phonologically independent word calques are entirely unrelated items calqued from English, as in the following example:

5)   "Corrió *para gobernador."* ["He *ran* for governor."]

In noncontact Spanish, the verb *correr* [to run] is not used metaphorically in the sense of "to seek elective office" as it is in English; this idea would more likely be expressed in a phrase such as *Se presentó como candidato para gobernador.*

Phrasal calques are word combinations that exist in Spanish but that are used in a new way in U.S. Spanish, because they are calqued from English. They are not unusual linguistically but are striking to persons from noncontact varieties of Spanish, because they convey meanings that are culturally appropriated from English. An example is the expression *lo último que necesito* (an obvious calque from the English expression, *the last thing I need*), which in noncontact varieties would more likely be expressed as *lo que me faltaría.*

Table 4.1 presents the frequency of loanwords and calques found in the 60 narratives sampled. Again, the analysis is performed on three groups who represent differing linguistic abilities: Spanish-dominant speakers (Group 1), bilingual speakers (Group 2) and English-dominant speakers (Group 3). The numbers and percentages indicated are of each type of borrowing out of the total borrowings per group.

For all groups, unintegrated loanwords are the most numerous type of borrowing. For Group 2 and 3, the phrasal calque is the type of borrowing that is second in frequency; these borrowings account for 24% of the Group 3 data and 19% of the Group 2 data. Unintegrated loanwords constitute almost 90% of all Group 1 borrowings. Each of the other types make up less than 5% of borrowings in Group 1 data.

The high percentage of unintegrated loanwords may be misleading because it includes an extremely high frequency of discourse markers (*so, you know, but, and*, etc.). Discourse markers account for 66% (76 of 115 responses) of all Group 3 unintegrated loanwords. They account for 53% (27 of 51 responses) of Group 2's and 14% (12 of 87 responses) of Group 1's unintegrated loanwords. Discourse markers serve to regulate the discourse by adding cohesive elements and, therefore, have a functional rather than purely lexical role. Because they do not have referential meaning, in the sense that nouns, verbs, adjectives, and adverbs do, they are excluded in what follows so that only signs with referential meaning are considered (I deal with discourse markers separately in a following section). Table 4.2 presents the results of the analysis excluding discourse markers from the unintegrated loanword category.

When discourse markers are excluded, a somewhat different picture emerges. The most common type of borrowing for Group 1 participants is still in the unintegrated loanword category; 86% of all their borrowing is accounted for in this way. All other types of borrowings each account for 6% or less of the total. Whereas unintegrated loanwords are also the most common type of borrowing for Group 2, words in this category now account for only 56% of all borrowings. These are followed by phrasal calques, which represent 30% of the total. In the Group 3 narratives, on the other hand, the most common form of borrowing is the use of phrasal

TABLE 4.1
Types of Borrowing

	Group 1		Group 2		Group 3	
Integrated Loanword	3%	(3)	4%	(3)	13%	(23)
Unintegrated Loanword	87%	(87)	72%	(51)	63%	(115)
Merged Calque	5%	(5)	2%	(1)	0%	(0)
Independent Calque	0%	(0)	3%	(2)	0%	(0)
Phrasal Calque	4%	(4)	19%	(13)	24%	(43)
Total Number of Borrowings	99		70		181	

TABLE 4.2
Types of Borrowing (Excluding Discourse Markers)

	Group 1		Group 2		Group 3	
Integrated Loanword	3%	(3)	56%	(24)	37%	(39)
Merged Calque	6%	(5)	2%	(1)	0%	(0)
Independent Calque	0%	(0)	5%	(2)	0%	(0)
Phrasal Calque	5%	(4)	30%	(13)	41%	(43)
Total Number of Borrowings	87		43		105	

calques, which account for 41% of all cases. These are followed by unintegrated loanwords, 37%, and integrated loanwords, 22%. Here we see very clear differences among the groups in the way English messages are incorporated into Spanish discourse at the word and phrasal level.

The most common method of integrating English for the Spanish-dominant speakers, Group 1, is through the use of unintegrated borrowing, almost exclusive of the other strategies. Groups 2 and 3, in contrast, rely on a range of innovative strategies, and Group 3 in particular uses three strategies—phrasal calques, unintegrated loanwords and integrated loanwords—with a frequency of more than 20% for each. Group 2 represents the middle of the road, in that similarly to Group 1, the most frequent strategy is the unintegrated loanword, but like Group 3, phrasal calques also constitute a much-used strategy. The English-dominant speakers use the borrowing strategies that demonstrate the most innovative integration of English into their discourse. Whereas the calquing strategies are based on English, they are originating new ways to use Spanish that may or may not be taken up by other speakers in the community.[4]

[4]It is interesting to compare these findings with the study of Cuban Spanish from which I derived the typology used here. The Otheguy and García (1988) study is based on a questionnaire distributed to 74 Cuban Americans living in Dade County. The questionnaire consists of sentences, some of which contained lexical innovations and others that did not. Respondents noted their awareness of innovative word usage in each sentence and indicated whether they would adopt the item and whether it was acceptable to them.

The investigators hypothesized that loanwords, which are most deviant compared to the various calques because they are most obviously taken from English, would be the least adopted and acceptable, and that phrasal calques, because they are least deviant, in the sense that lexically they are more like traditional Spanish, would be most adopted and acceptable. The results, however, indicated that loadwords are the most likely borrowings to be adopted, followed closely by phrasal calques. Although loanwords are judged to be most unacceptable, they are the most common. When interviewed, the participants said that ease of expression, and demands of communication, account for their incorporation of loanwords, the most unacceptable type of borrowing. The authors reason that loanwords and phrasal calques are adopted frequently because, in both casses, the integrity between meaning and sign is preserved. My findings concur somewhat with the results of the Otheguy and García (1988) questionnaire. Taken together, integrated and unintegrated loanwords account for 70% of all the borrowing in the data of all three groups combined. Loanwords are followed by phrasal calques, which account for a distant 25% of the borrowings. Together, merged and independent calques make up the other 5% of the borrowings.

In the Brentwood Puerto Rican sample, Spanish-dominant speakers (Group 1) adopt more loanwords than the bilinguals, Group 2 and Group 3, but the latter two rely more on calquing as a borrowing technique than does Group 1 (see Table 4.3).

This is intriguing in light of the fact that other linguists (Fries & Pike, 1949; Haugen, 1969) suggest that bilinguals are more likely to incorporate loanwords than monolinguals and integrate loanwords into the recipient language sooner than monolinguals. In my data, as dominance in Spanish decreases and English use increases, there is more calquing (especially phrasal calquing) and less use of loanwords.[5] That more options are utilized by Groups 2 and 3 is expected, given that they have two linguistic repertoires from which to draw. Group 1 members are limited in their borrowing strategies; although they are less familiar with English, they are less likely to translate English messages into Spanish. If they lack a word or phrase they are most likely to simply render it in English. For example, in the following segment of a Group 1 narrative (Text 4-A), the speaker resorts to the use of English loanwords 8 times—in lines 7, 8, and 9. She also uses a phonologically merged calque (*registra/registrado*) in lines 2 and 3. This latter type of borrowing is more typical of bilingual and English-dominant speakers.

Text 4-A

1) *la mamá va*
2) *y registra al niño*
3) entonce ehte tenemos cierta cantidad de niños registrados para empezar en septiembre
4) pueh, antes de ese niño empezal
5) tienen que venil
6) y hacele un . . . ¿qué se llama esto?
7) o sea son *diferentes* screening, el develop-developmental *eh* screening y el hearing screening
8) y así todas esas cosa, velda, el vision, todo eso . . . el screening test . . . el, la blood test, el urine test, todo eso
9) tonce, el el año pasado, no podían conseguir un chofer para el hearing van
10) y pasó el tiempo.

(Translation of narrative—italicized portions were produced in English, the rest of the text was produced in Spanish)

---

[5]Otheguy and García (1988) also conclude that the Spanish of the monolingual Spanish speakers in their sample demonstrates more influence from English than the Spanish of the bilinguals, because monolinguals report adopting innovations at a higher rate than bilinguals; monolinguals also judge English-influenced lexical items to be more acceptable than do bilingual speakers.

participation. In the following section from a Group 3 narrative (Text 4-D), the function of the English language discourse markers in all three categories can be seen. In the narrative, a young woman explains how she fought back when she was discriminated against by an employer:

Text 4-D

1) *cuando yo fui a la oficina*
2) *ella vio que* . . . you know . . . *yo era puertorriqueña*
3) *no era lo que ella esperaba*
4) *y me dijo*
5) *que ya* . . . *habían cogido el trabajo ya*
6) *pero yo cogí*
7) *fui a donde mi tía*
8) *que ella, como te dije la última vez,*
9) *pelea por todo*
10) *ella, si tien—si ella ve algo*
11) *que no está* right *o algo*
12) *pelea*
13) so *ella fue*
14) and *me llevó a* small claims court
15) *que es donde uno va*
16) *cuando es discriminando,* y' know
17) *y, este, ella fue*
18) *y, este, como la muchacha dijo*
19) *que me había entrenado*
20) *ya había, ya ya me había entrenado*
21) so *era* . . . *es* . . . *quería decir, sí*
22) *que yo tenía el trabajo*
23) so *ella fue a la corte con nosotros*
24) *y gracias a dioh*
25) *como ella dijo*
26) *que, que, que ya me había entrenado*
27) *y eso quería decir* y' know
28) *que yo tenía trabajo,*
29) *pues me tuvieron que dar el trabajo*

[1] when I went to the office
2) she saw that . . . *you know* I was Puerto Rican
3) it wasn't what she expected
4) and she said to me,
5) that already . . . they had taken the job already
6) but I took
7) I went to my aunt
8) that she, like I told you last time

9)   she fights for everything
10)   she, if she has—if she sees something
11)   that's not right or something
12)   she fights
13)   *so* she went
14)   *and* she took me to small claims court
15)   which is where one goes
16)   when one is discriminated, *you know*
17)   and, ummm, she went
18)   and ummm because the girl said
19)   that she had already trained me
20)   already had, she had already already trained me
21)   *so* it was . . . is . . . it meant, yes
22)   that I had the job
23)   *so* she went to the court with us
24)   and thank God
25)   because she said
26)   that, that, that they had already trained me
27)   and that meant *y' know*
28)   that I had the job
29)   well they had to give me the job]

In this 29-line section of a longer oral narrative, the English-dominant speaker uses six English discourse markers. Three markers are the participation marker *y' know* in lines 2, 16, and 27. They occur at crucial places in her story where the narrator apparently wanted to ensure that I was following her story. In line 2, she wants to make sure that I was following exactly why the employer found her unacceptable even after she had been trained for the job. In line 16, she seeks to ensure that I understood why her aunt "took her" to small claims court—because she had been discriminated against. And in line 27, she wants to ensure that I understand that the fact that she had already been trained meant that she should have the job she applied for. The narrator also uses the discourse marker, *so*, to indicate a result in lines 13, 21, and 23. She further uses the connective *and* in line 14 to join two clauses.

In my data, discourse markers constitute a full 41% of all loanwords. As noted before, the frequency of English language discourse markers increases dramatically as knowledge of English increases. As Table 4.4 shows, discourse markers account for 66% of all the single word borrowings for Group 3, 53% for Group 2, and only 14% for Group 1, the Spanish-dominant group. That discourse markers figure so dramatically as loanwords in my Group 2 and Group 3 data is surprising in light of the fact that Weinreich (1953) claims that morphemes such as inflections and function words are less likely to be borrowed than content words such as nouns and verbs; however, the present study shows that as bilingual ability increases, so does the likelihood that function words will be borrowed. In another study, Mougean et al. (1985) argue that borrowing of core lexical items such as discourse markers is associated with situations of intense language contact. They analyze the use of *so* in the discourse of Canadian bilingual adolescents, whom they categorize as either low, mid-, or high users of French. They discover that midlevel users of French use *so* more frequently than others. The authors deduce from this that balanced bilingualism is probably a prerequisite for the borrowing of core lexical items to take place. They suggest that speakers who identify English as the prestige language use *so* to signal that they have knowledge of the language of power. They also propose that borrowing of core lexical items could be taken as an indicator of balanced bilingualism.

My data similarly indicate that as proficiency in a second language increases, so does the level of borrowing of core lexical items, because the use of discourse markers becomes significant for Groups 2 and 3, the groups who have a greater degree of bilingual ability. For both these groups, discourse markers represent more than 50% of all the single word borrowings incorporated in their speech. Although English discourse markers are also present in the Group 1 data, they represent only 14% of their single word borrowings.

To place the data in context, we must compare the use of discourse markers in Spanish and English. Specifically, we must consider how likely it is that a particular category will be produced in Spanish versus English by a Brentwood speaker. Table 4.5 presents the combined distribution of all English and Spanish discourse markers in my data.

Comparing the use of English and Spanish markers in Table 4.5, we see that all groups overwhelmingly favor the Spanish language connectives studied here, *y* and *pero* [*and* and *but*]; this is not surprising given that speakers are producing Spanish language narratives and *y* is a common connective to move stories along in Spanish. In terms of the cause and result markers, *entonces* and *porque* [*so* and *because*], Group 1 favors the Spanish markers by a 6 to 1 ratio, whereas Group 2 favors the Spanish markers by a ratio of 2 to 1 and Group 3 speakers are nearly as likely to choose an English or Spanish marker to express relations of cause and effect. The trend suggests that, as Spanish dominance decreases, so does the use of Spanish cause and effect markers, although both Groups 2 and 3 have at least an even facility with regard to use of this marker. Of the two cause and effect English language markers studied, *so* is used more frequently by all groups. Given the increase in the use of this marker for Groups 2 and 3, perhaps here, as in the French situation discussed earlier (Mougean et al., 1985), the case can be made that, as bilingual ability increases, so does the borrowing of core lexical items such as discourse markers, particularly

TABLE 4.5
Discourse Markers in English and Spanish

Types	Group 1						Group 2						Group 3					
	English		Spanish		Total		English		Spanish		Total		English		Spanish		Total	
Connectives	1%	(3)	99%	(281)	284		5%	(10)	95%	(176)	186		7%	(23)	93%	(296)	319	
Cause/effect	6%	(7)	94%	(112)	119		31%	(26)	69%	(58)	84		49%	(68)	51%	(70)	138	
Participation	50%	(13)	50%	(13)	26		64%	(9)	36%	(5)	14		76%	(75)	24%	(24)	99	

those that carry the most semantic weight. It is also interesting to note that the Group 1 participant who most uses *so* in her speech is the Spanish-dominant person who has the best grasp of English; this fact confirms the findings of the aforementioned study.

With regard to participation markers, *sabes* and *digo* [*y'know* and *I mean*], all groups use English markers at least 50% of the time. Group 2 prefers English language participation markers by a 2 to 1 margin and Group 3 prefers them by a 3 to 1 margin (see Table 4.5). For two groups (Groups 2 and 3) they are the least frequently used Spanish language discourse maker and the most frequently used English language discourse marker. Interestingly, they function differently in each set of narratives. Fifty-six percent of all the English language discourse markers produced by the Spanish-dominant group (Group 1) fall into the participation category (*y'know* and *I mean*). It seems likely that of all discourse markers, the Spanish-dominant group would first incorporate this type into their speech, because they have little semantic content. In fact, rather than being used to ensure attention (as it is used in the Group 3 data), the marker is often used in Group 1 narratives in order to signal that the narrator is changing languages, if only for a brief time. For example, in the following continuation of Text 4-A produced by a Group 1 speaker, the narrator signals a code-mixed sequence twice by using the discourse marker *y' know*:

Text 4-E

1) *pero en ese* hearing van *ellos tienen un equipo muy bueno*
2) *y entonces no pudimos tener ese* hearing van
3) *hasta . . . cuando fue . . . mayo,* y'know of 1989 or March
4) *y ya* y'know it's almost the end
5) *casi es el final del, del año*

[1) but in that hearing van they have good equipment
2) and then we were unable to have that hearing van
3) until . . . when was it . . . May, *y'know of 1989 or March*
4) and already *y'know it's almost the end*
5) it's almost the end of, of the year]

Most Spanish-dominant speakers used participation markers this way and in a very different manner from that of English-dominant speakers. As we have seen (Text 4-C), for English-dominant speakers, these markers do not involve transition from Spanish to English but rather appear to serve mainly an interactional function to insure the attention and participation of the listener of the narrative. Group 2, the bilingual group, uses participation markers for both functions. It may be that Group 3 speakers rely on participation markers, especially English discourse markers, given that they are telling stories in their less dominant language and want to check frequently and make sure that the listener is following the narratives.

Thus, we see that, in Brentwood, although all Puerto Ricans in the study use the same range of discourse markers in their speech, each group follows its own patterns; and sometimes the same discourse markers function quite differently in their oral narratives.

CODE-MIXING IN THE NARRATIVES

In addition to borrowing, code-mixing is often associated with U.S. Spanish varieties. Numerous studies demonstrate that code-mixing, the alternation of two or more languages in the same utterance, is a common phenomenon in bilingual situations (Grosjean, 1982; Heller, 1988). Despite its prevalence, as shown in chapter 2, whereas more than 75% of all survey participants acknowledge code-mixing, more than 50% feel that code-mixing is a negative behavior. Most participants claim that they do not know why they code-mix.

Various authors have studied the use of code-mixing in the narratives of Spanish–English bilinguals (Koike, 1987; Silva-Corvalán, 1988; Valdés, 1976). Whereas Valdés (1976) and Koike (1987) highlight the use of code-mixing as a means of narrative evaluation, Silva-Corvalán (1988) points out that, for speakers on the lower end of the bilingual continuum, code-mixing is used primarily to fill lexical gaps. Silva-Corvalán (1983a) introduces the term *code-shifting* to refer to the strategy used by English-dominant speakers when they encounter problems while speaking Spanish. The shift from Spanish to English is not for creative purposes; the speaker is not engaging in this behavior as an optional discourse move but to fill a lexical gap. It is relevant to question how the investigator can distinguish between code-mixing to fulfill a creative, deliberate discourse function, and code-mixing (shifting) to fill a lexical gap. In Silva-Corvalán's data, pauses, hesitations, and meta-linguistic comments (i.e., "How do you say that?") signal code-shifting. These are good indicators that speakers are resorting to code-shifting as defined by Silva-Corvalán. However, the use of code-mixing itself does not necessarily indicate a lack of knowledge of a language. Poplack (1982b) suggests just the opposite, that it is those community members who have a very good familiarity with both Spanish and English who will most likely engage in code-mixing. In the Puerto Rican community she studied the speakers who most participated in intrasentential code-mixing were those who were most proficient in both languages. Thus, Poplack (1982) proposes that the use of code-mixing can be a gauge of bilingual ability in a stable bilingual community.

I analyze here code-mixing as a discourse move that some speakers use strategically to enhance their narratives. Labov (1972) and others

(Romaine, 1984) state that differences exist between the narratives produced by adults and children, related to the adults' superior competence in the language. Labov (1972) finds, for example, that such strategic narrative devices as intensifiers (for example quantifiers) and correlatives (which bring together two events that occur simultaneously) are virtually absent from the stories of younger narrators. Given that dominance in the Spanish language decreases across the three groups of Puerto Ricans studied here (the first group is Spanish-dominant, the second is bilingual, and the third is dominant in English), I consider the following hypothesis: There is differential use of code-mixing across the three groups. The bilingual group uses code-mixing as an optional discourse strategy to enhance the narrative; the use of code-mixing is specifically related to the different components of the narrative. The other two groups use code-mixing to fill lexical gaps, in other words, as an obligatory discourse move rather than as an optional, creative discourse strategy.

CODE-MIXING: AN OPTIONAL OR OBLIGATORY DISCOURSE STRATEGY

All Puerto Rican speakers in the Brentwood study have several discourse strategies in common, although their frequency and function vary according to the group. For the purposes of this analysis, I first discuss code-mixing at the clausal level, considering those cases in which the speaker produces an entire clause in English. Code-mixing at the clausal level is a strategy employed by all speakers but it is employed rather differently. The narratives of Group 1, the Spanish-dominant Puerto Ricans, have the fewest cases in which speakers switch an entire clause; these account for 2.7% of the clauses. Group 2 switches to English for 5.3% of their clauses, whereas the English-dominant Puerto Ricans, Group 3, produces 9.5% of all their clauses in English. Mixing above the word level but less than the entire clause is also quantified. Here again, as expected, the most frequent mixing is found in the narratives of Group 3. In 4% of their clauses there is mixing greater than at the word level but less than at the level of the entire clause. This is true for .8% of the Group 2 data and .6% of the Group 1 data. Thus, overall, whereas all speakers code-mix to various degrees, code-mixing in the oral narratives of the Brentwood Puerto Rican community is not as frequent as one might expect.[6]

Group 1, the Spanish-dominant group, only superficially uses code-mixing as a creative discourse strategy. Most of the English in their

---

[6]It may also be that the research situation (an interview with an academic) may have inhibited code-switching.

narratives can be classified as borrowing because it occurs at the word level. Most of these instances are words related to specialized lexical areas. Many of the alternations to English occur in those narratives where the participant is talking about work or situations that occur in the public domain. For example, in the following section of a narrative (Text 4-F), a male social worker from Group 1 begins to explain how he secured his previous job:

Text 4-F

1) *fui aquí un día al, al* Labor Department
2) *y, y, y por coincidencia conseguí un trabajo de trabajador social*
3) *trabajé para el* Heat Department
4) *el* Heat Department *is un programa de energía*
5) *es para la gente, de aceite*
6) *ellos te ayudan a pagar el aceite*
7) *para personas que se viven de servicio social*
8) *y, este, para gente también* senior citizen
9) *que son gente*
10) *que tienen su propia casa*
11) *pero que el cheque de seguro social y eso no le es suficiente*
12) *pues es como un* grant
13) *que da el, el, el estado para ellos*

[1) I came here one day to the *Labor Department*
2) and, and, and by coincidence I got a job as a social worker
3) I worked for the *Heat Department*
4) The *Heat Department is* an energy program
5) it's for people, of oil
6) they help you pay the oil
7) for people who live from social services
8) and also for people *senior citizens*
9) who are people
10) who have their own house
11) but that social services check and that isn't enough for them
12) well it's like a *grant*
13) that the, the, the state gives them]

In this narrative, the following English words are uttered: Labor Department, Heat Program, senior citizen, and grant. These and other words are sprinkled throughout the complete narrative, but they are not found to be more numerous in any discourse component (i.e., abstract, evaluation, complicating action, etc.) and do not seem to be serving a creative, optional discourse function. Rather, the items represent words that are related to, and were most likely learned, in English-speaking settings such as the work place. Because they are specialized words, speakers would probably be hard-pressed to give the Spanish equivalents of such lexical items; thus, the obligatory alternation to English. This is the case in all Group 1 mixing at the word level (see also Text 4-A).

As we have seen in the last section, when Group 1 speakers use the discourse marker of participation they also tend to code-mix for at least a portion of the adjacent clause. However, the majority of the full clause switches to English in the Group 1 data do have an optional discourse function; they are instances of direct speech. The speakers indicate that these quoted utterances were delivered in English. In the following narrative (Text 4-G), about a man lost in a school building on his arrival to New York, there is this optional use of code-mixing in lines 23 and 27:

> Text 4-G

1) *cuando me pusieron en esa clase, todos americanos*
2) *yo era el único latino*
3) *y no sabía nada de inglés, nada, nada, absolutamente nada*
4) *y me acuerdo*
5) *que una vez me perdí en la escuela*
6) *y, este, en aquellos tiempos tenían reglah la ehcuela*
7) *habían unas escalerah*
8) *que eran* up *y otras* down
9) *uno tenía que buhcal la la ehcalera*
10) *que dijeran* down
11) *y no podía mete—bajar para abajo*
12) *donde decía* up
13) *polque ahí pueh ya lo* monitors
14) *que tenían en aquel tiempo*
15) *empujaban a uno*
16) *y que sé yo*
17) *y yo perdío*
18) *bajándome*
19) *subiéndome por la ehcalera de* down
20) *y entonces me hablaban*
21) *y yo loh miraba*
22) *y al último yo dije*
23) "I wan' room one two seven"
24) *era el, el salón mío*
25) *era* one twenty seven
26) *y dehpuéh me dijeron*
27) "Oh, one twenty seven, okay come on"
28) *entonces me llevaron al salón*
29) *pero fue bien difícil*

[1)   when they put me in that class, all Americans
2)   I was the only Latino
3)   and I didn't know any English, nothing, nothing absolutely nothing
4)   and I remember
5)   that once I got lost in the school
6)   and umm, in those times they had rules in the school
7)   there were stairs
8)   that were up and others were *down*
9)   one had to look for the stairs
10)   that said *down*
11)   and you couldn't get—go down
12)   where it said *up*
13)   because there well already the *monitors*
14)   that they had in that time
15)   pushed people
16)   and what do I know
17)   and me lost
18)   going down
19)   going up the *down* staircase
20)   and then they talked to me
21)   and I would look at them
22)   and finally I said
23)   *"I wan' room one two seven"*
24)   it was my classroom
25)   it was *one twenty seven*
26)   and then they said
27)   *"oh, one twenty seven, okay, come on"*
28)   then they took me to the classroom
29)   but it was really difficult]

The speaker narrates that, after wandering in the wrong staircase in frustration, he explains to a hall monitor in his limited English, "I wan' room one two seven." The monitor's response is also reproduced in English. Although the narrator produced these utterance in English when telling the narrative, he had the option of reproducing these quotes in either language. In terms of his narration, uttering these statements in English more closely matches the actual event remembered and therefore added more dramatic realism than would have been the case had they been reproduced in Spanish.

The majority of all code-mixing for Groups 2 and 3 occurs in the evaluation components of the narratives. More than 50% of all code-mixing takes place in this section for both the bilingual and the English-dominant groups. In the evaluation sections, the narrator expresses why the narrative is worth telling. The use of English here serves a dramatizing effect (Koike, 1987); as in the foregoing example, the speaker switches languages to emphasize a portion of the text.

The use of code-mixing to serve this particular function is seen in the narrative about the near rape presented in chapter 3 (Text 3-A, pp. 38–40). The Group 3 narrator tells a dramatic story about narrowly escaping a rape when she and her friend accept a ride from acquaintances. In line 19, she interrupts the narrative to evaluate the story by commenting on the action in English. Lines 24–26 are another example of the use of code-mixing for evaluating. The speaker is at the point of highest tension in the narrative; she then suspends the action to deliver a 3-clause evaluation, which she offers in English to create a dramatic effect. Again in line 34, the narrator switches from Spanish to English to evaluate the danger she and her friend are in; she accomplishes this by presenting her friend's fear. In each case, shifting to English captures the listener's attention by adding a heightened dimension of emphasis through the distancing effected by the switch.

The following narrative (Text 4-H) produced by a Group 2 speaker demonstrates another case in which the evaluation is produced in English for similar reasons. In this narrative, the speaker tells the story of how she became motivated to learn English after being insulted by an Anglo boy.

Text 4-H

1) *yo hablaba máh que español*
2) *y te voy a decir a tí una cosa*
3) *tenía un muchachito que se sentaba al lado mío*
4) *que se llamaba* Kevin McReynolds,
5) *creo que era*
6) *y ese muchacho era amigo mío toda la vida*
7) *hahta que supo que yo era latina*
8) *entonceh ese día vino a la escuela*
9) *y se sentó al lado de mí*
10) "you dirty spic"
11) *pero como yo no entendía mucho inglés*
12) *yo creía que tenía que escupir*—spit
13) *y saqué mi galgao y (ja ja)*
14) *dijo,* "uh she spit at me"
15) *verdad,* that goes to show you
16) but you know *que causó una impresión en mi vida*
17) *porque me dio bochorno*
18) *porque me di cuenta que no le había entendido*
19) *que después de eso yo me forcé a aprender inglés*
20) *pero* Kevin *que me enseñó*

21)   *cuando dijo "you dirty spic"*
22)   *(humm) . . . él tenía el pelo colorao*
23)   *y tenía muchah pequitah*
24)   *yo decía pero mira pa'ya que bruta yo*
25)   *si no me ha dicho nada de escupir,*
26)   *pero pa'que bochorno*
27)   *y el bochorno me dio coraje suficiente para aprender inglés*

[1)   I spoke only Spanish
2)   and I'm going to tell you something
3)   I had this kid who sat next to me
4)   who was named Kevin McReynolds
5)   I think it was
6)   and the kid was a friend of mine all of my life
7)   until he found out I was Latina
8)   then one day he came to school
9)   and he sat down next to me
10)   *"you dirty spic"*
11)   but because I didn't understand much English
12)   I thought I had to spit—*spit*
13)   and I got ready to and (makes spitting noise)
14)   he said, *"uh she spit at me"*
15)   right, *that goes to show you*
16)   *but you know*, that, it made an impression on my life
17)   because it made me ashamed
18)   because I realized that I hadn't understood
19)   and after that I forced myself to learn English
20)   but Kevin showed me
21)   when he said,*"you dirty spic"*
22)   (humm) . . . he had red hair
23)   and had a lot of freckles
24)   I said but look at that how stupid I am
25)   he hadn't said anything to me about spitting
26)   but what shame
27)   and the shame made me angry enough to learn English]

In line 10, this Group 2 speaker switches to English to quote the insult
that was leveled at her in English; this quote functions as the most
significant part of the complicating action. Then the narrator repeats
this phrase in a separate evaluation section on line 21, again quoting it
directly to dramatize it. Line 21 forms part of an evaluative sequence
that can also be used to demonstrate another common use of code-mixing
in the Group 2 data. In lines 15–20, the speaker offers an evaluation in
the narrative; she signals that she is moving to another section of the

narrative by turning from Spanish to English. The evaluation then continues in Spanish until the speaker closes the evaluation section by switching to English. In line 22 she returns to Spanish, producing another orientation section and then providing the resolution of the narrative. This optional discourse function, the use of code-mixing to mark or bracket off a particular component of the narrative, is a frequent strategy used by Group 2 speakers.

As seen already, another common use of code-mixing is to reproduce direct speech from the narrator or another participant in the story. Whereas all groups use this strategy, Group 3 speakers employ this technique much more frequently than do Group 2 members, and this is the only case in which a Group 1 member switches to English at the clause level.

Interestingly, in many of Group 3's narratives, the same speaker is presented as speaking first in one language then in the other. It is not clear from the narratives whether the paraphrased material was originally delivered in Spanish or English. For example, in the Group 3 narrative about the near rape presented in chapter 3 (Text 3-A), the narrator's comments to her interlocutors are sometimes expressed in Spanish (lines 15, 16, 18, and 28–33) and sometimes in English (lines 14, 21, and 37); the same is true for the comments her interlocutors make to her throughout the narrative. The narrator indicates that the other speakers are Black Americans and, although possible, it is improbable that the interlocutors are also bilingual. The presentation of the narrator's mixing of Spanish and English in the narrative reflects the naturalness of bilingualism in her own speech and the knowledge that her listener is bilingual. However, the alternation of languages in the dialogue of her American interlocutors is more questionable. Whereas some researchers argue that alternating languages may be a strategy employed to mark a contrast between the different voices in the narrative (Koike, 1987), this clearly does not occur in Text 3-A and the other Group 3 narratives, because all the interlocutors are presented as alternating between the languages.

As can be seen, narrative code-mixing occurs in every component of Group 3's data, and it is often difficult to assign a specific discourse purpose to each switch. Code-mixing also takes place in all components of Group 1 data, but in this case mixing, like borrowing, is used primarily to produce technical, lexical items for which the speakers probably do not have other terms; this is an obligatory discourse function. These speakers infrequently code-mix to reproduce direct speech, although as noted in some of the texts just discussed, this does happen. In Group 2 narratives, mixing is used for evaluations, direct speech, and to signal a shift from one section of the narrative to another; all these are optional discourse functions.

Also, whereas Group 2 uses code-mixing sparingly for some very defined functions in specific sections of the narrative, Group 3 narrators use the device not only to produce evaluations or to quote a speaker; but also to fill a lexical gap. Examples of this are seen in the following Group 3 narrative (Text 4-I):

Text 4-I

1) *Yo tenía quince años*
2) so *ya yo tenía mi mente entiende*
3) *y en ese tiempo yo estaba endroga y to eso*
4) so *yo había bregao con mucha gente que eran major, tú sabe*
5) so *nunca eh—yo nunca—lah personah que yo jangeaba trataron de*—take advantage of me *nunca*
6) cause *yo siempre ha tenido la mente, entiende*
7) *pero con mi tío*
8) *cuando mi papá se fue*
9) *yo siempre ha tratado de buscar alguien para*—to replace, *entiende*
10) so *mi tío estaba* right next door
11) so *me sentía bien, tú sabe,*—comfortable, *con él*
12) so I wouldn't mind, you know
13) *pero cuando él se trató de poner frehco conmigo*
14) *eso me dolió tanto*
15) *polque yo trohté en él*
16) *tú sabe yo no pensaba que él iba a ser una cosa así*
17) *y yo fui*
18) *y volé*
19) *y se lo dije a mi mai, rápidito*
20) and I really *yo yo lo hice sentir bien mal*
21) *cuando eso pasó yo hablé con él* right in my mother's face
22) *y yo le dije,*
23) *"yo no puedo creer que tú me hiciste una—traté de hacerme una cosa así*
24) *yo trohtaba en ti*
25) *que clase de hombre tú eres*
26) *si mi papá el hago, le hace algo así a tu hija*
27) *¿cómo te vas a sentir tú?*
28) *eso no está bien*
29) *¿qué tú no puedes ir por allí a encontrar crica hum?"*
30) I'm serious
31) I broke
32) I went crazy *y estaba llorando y to'*
33) *eso—un rebolú*
34) *pero por eso yo hablo de eso con los niños.*

[1)   I was 15
2)   *so* I already had my mind, you understand
3)   and at that time I was involved in drugs and all of that
4)   *so* I had dealt with a lot of people that were older, you know
5)   *so* never—I never—the people I hung out with tried to *take advantage of me* never
6)   *cause* I also had my mind, understand
7)   but with my uncle
8)   when my father left
9)   I always tried to find someone to—*to replace*, understand
10)   *so* my uncle was *right next door*
11)   *so* I felt good, you know, *comfortable*, with him
12)   *so I wouldn't mind, you know*
13)   but when he tried to get fresh with me
14)   that hurt me so much
15)   because I trusted in him
16)   you know I never thought he was gonna do something like that
17)   so I went
18)   I flew
19)   and I told my mother, quickly
20)   *and I really* I I made him feel really bad
21)   when that happened I spoke with him *right in my mother's face*
22)   and I told him,
23)   "I can't believe you did such a thing—tried to do such a thing like that
24)   I trusted in you
25)   What kind of man are you
26)   if my father does something like that to your daughter
27)   how are you gonna feel?
28)   that's not right
29)   What, can't go out and get some pussy huh?"
30)   *I'm serious*
31)   *I broke*
32)   *I went crazy* and was crying and everything
33)   that—a mess
34)   but because of that I talk about that with the kids.]

In line 5 the speaker pauses and hesitates as if groping for the phrase in Spanish and then produces an ungrammatical construction in Spanish completed by an infinitive structure in English. In line 9, the speaker refers to her search for a father figure. Here a pause followed by an English infinitive verb form signals that the narrator alternates languages because of a lexical gap. On the other hand, this speaker clearly also uses code-mixing as an optional discourse function when she delivers an emotional three line dramatic evaluation of the situation in lines 30–32. Spanish and English, in general, are mixed in the entire transcripts of the Spanish language oral narratives of English-dominant speakers.

CONCLUSION

Kachru (1985) argues that when studying bilingual speech, we must make a distinction between *deficiency* and *difference*. Along the bilingual continuum (Silva Corvalán, 1988) or the cline of bilingualism (Kachru, 1985), what, at one stage may be an example of a lexical gap, at another stage (or even at another instance for the same speaker) may be an innovation or a creative optional use of borrowing or code-mixing. The use of borrowing strategies which involve calquing, for example, is an area where Group 3 participants are involved in creative language production in Spanish. The borrowing of items from a range of grammatical categories is another example of creative language usage by bilingual and English-dominant speakers.

The use of code-mixing across the three groups studied seems more complicated than suggested by my original hypothesis. The Spanish-dominant group, Group 1, resorts to code-mixing, as well as borrowing, primarily to fill lexical gaps. Whereas in a few cases this is marked by hesitations or pauses, most of the time the switch is fluently integrated into the discourse. Because borrowings are for the most part technical, work-related words or phrases, they are probably the only terms in the speakers' lexicon for the items. The majority of the discourse markers integrated into the speech of Puerto Rican Spanish dominant speakers function primarily to mark a switch to English and have little semantic content.

Code-mixing is most unambiguously identifiable as a creative discourse function in the narratives of the Group 2 bilingual speakers. In this case, there seems to be a clear relationship between the use of code-mixing and optional discourse purposes. This group appears to use code-mixing strategically to accomplish certain discourse goals; specifically, code-mixing is used as one type of evaluation device, as a way to reproduce direct quotes, and in order to signal a transition from one narrative component to the next. There are no cases in which mixing seemed to be precipitated by a lexical gap. For Group 2, most of the English language discourse markers used are those that do have a semantic meaning.

Group 3 uses code-mixing for both optional and obligatory discourse functions. Optional mixing occurs in an evaluation function in approximately 50% of the cases in which it appears. It is also evident, however, that speakers are additionally resorting to code-mixing when they are unable to think of a word in Spanish. This obligatory function, to fill lexical gaps, is signaled by hesitations, pauses, and resulting awkward constructions that violate the grammatical structure of Spanish, or English, or both. Unlike the case of Group 1 borrowings, which are for the most part, technical terms, Group 3 speakers borrow a broad range of lexical and grammatical items into their speech.

There is thus a progression in the narratives. Group 1 speakers use code-mixing and borrowing to fill lexical gaps. The switching of discourse markers does not involve those in English that have discourse properties as well as grammatical functions; rather, only those without serious semantic weight are used. Group 2 uses code-mixing primarily as a strategic discourse device to achieve specific discourse purposes. The markers that are switched are those that have semantic weight. Group 3, the English-dominant group, prefers creative borrowing strategies, for example, the use of phrasal calquing. They use code-mixing both creatively, to dramatize portions of the text, or to present direct quotes, and as a crutch, when their Spanish speaking ability is limited.

This progression suggests that, although Spanish language attrition may be underway for Group 3 members, they are able to use their total language skills effectively and innovatively. It is true that some of the youngest narrators, the teenagers born and raised in Brentwood, may be losing their Spanish-speaking ability. Most speakers in Group 3 claim that although their mother tongue is Spanish, once they entered the school system they began to speak primarily in English. They use Spanish mainly to speak to their parents and to other Spanish monolingual friends and relatives. On the other hand, some Brentwood Puerto Rican young people, involved in jobs or with the church where they are in contact with recent arrivals or older Latinos, have noticed a reactivation of their Spanish-speaking ability. Consistent involvement in Spanish-speaking networks seems to be the crucial factor in maintaining Spanish language use. The current situation suggests that English-dominant Puerto Rican speakers still can and do use Spanish effectively. As we have seen, whereas they engage in much English-language borrowing and code-mixing, they also use borrowing strategies that entail manipulating the Spanish language in original and creative ways, for example, by calquing English language ideas into an original Spanish version. They sometimes use code-mixing to fill lexical gaps, but they are also able to use this discourse strategy innovatively, to a certain degree along the same lines as the Group 2 speakers.

The results of this study of Spanish language oral narratives of Brentwood Puerto Ricans suggest that the perception that the Spanish of U.S. Latinos is marked by very frequent use of English is exaggerated. The misconception that the Spanish of Latinos is heavily influenced by English is probably due to what Poplack (1982a) characterizes as "categorical perception," as she explains this: "The emphasis on

anomalies in multilingual situations on the part of researchers, educators, and intellectuals, is merely stereotyping due the phenomenon of
categorical perception, whereby deviation from a norm may be seen as
far more prominent than its negligible frequency would warrant"
(Poplack, 1982a, pp. 21–22). In Brentwood, as we have seen, the frequency of English used in the Spanish language narratives is modest.
English single-word borrowings account for only 1.9% of the total word
output of the narratives. Mixing greater than at the word level accounts
for less than 1% for Groups 1 and 2, and 5% for Group 3. At the clause
level, no group switches to English for more than 10% of their clauses.
Although for Group 3 there is a significant increase in mixing over
Groups 1 and 2, overall the amount of English in the narratives is
surprisingly minimal. These results suggest that the Puerto Rican
Spanish-dominant, bilingual, and English-dominant community members in Brentwood continue to use and maintain a Spanish that retains
its grammatical and lexical integrity as it incorporates innovation in its
new multilingual environment. English-dominant Puerto Ricans, because of their continued interactions with Spanish-dominant speakers
and their participation in situations that require that they negotiate
both Spanish and English, retain their ability to use Spanish in ways
that are both similar to and different from other community members.

Having considered grammatical and structural features of the narratives, in the next chapter, I turn to an analysis of the content of the
stories, which focuses on the internalization of and resistance to mainstream ideology about race and gender by Brentwood Puerto Rican
speakers.

5

Language and Power
in Puerto Rican Oral Narratives

This chapter examines oral narratives in Brentwood to investigate how Puerto Ricans construct their social selves through discourse about themselves and their communities.[1] In the course of the interviews I conducted with each participant on Latino life in the United States, I elicited community perspectives on language, identity, and gender issues. The stories produced in these exchanges provide the basis for a discussion of the internalization of and resistance to racism and sexism in the community, as well as the linguistic and rhetorical strategies speakers use to convey a multifaceted discourse.

The narratives that people tell embody a rich source of social and cultural information. Polanyi (1985) claims that an analysis of the everyday narratives people share in the United States reveals an "American Story" (p. 4). She studies the linguistic and social constraints that condition the narratives told by White, middle-class speakers. Van Dijk (1993) explains that *stories* are representations of episodic (mental) models that people are constantly updating as they interpret and reinterpret the events and situations of their lives. Stories have a sociocultural function in that they are one important way in which knowledge is reproduced in the culture and societal ideologies, beliefs, and norms are propagated. Narratives reveal the values, goals, and identities that have been internalized; they illustrate the characteristics around which group solidarity is expressed and others are differentiated. Linde (1993) argues that speakers use stories to assert or negotiate group membership and to demonstrate that they are worthy members of the associations they belong to and that they properly adhere to their "moral standards."

---

[1]The few studies on U.S. Puerto Rican discourse that inform this project are Alvarez (1988), Bennet & Pedraza (1988), and Ruskin & Varenne (1983). Through a study of discourse strategies and linguistic features, these studies suggest methodologies to interpret community narratives and the production of other types of discourse. Through a comparison of American and Puerto Rican discourse, Ruskin & Varenne (1983), for example, find differences in the organizational features of narratives for the two groups.

An issue that particularly interested me as I studied the narratives was the structuring of internalized oppression in the community. Allport (1958), in his classic study of prejudice, analyzes its effects on victims of discrimination. Among other traits associated with victimization, Allport names *self-hatred* as common to oppressed groups. He argues that self-hatred is motivated by the Western sentiment of individualism, an ideology that presumes that each person is responsible for her fate, so that if she is hated, it must be her own fault. In a similar vein, Yamato (1990) argues that certain racial and ethnic groups internalize racism because they are continually being discriminated against and beaten down. This constant, day-to-day assault leads affected groups to believe that the abuse they receive is deserved, to accept abuse as just the way things are, or to minimize or deny its existence.

Similar processes are at work when women internalize sexism (hooks, 1984, 1993; Moraga, 1983; Rich, 1983). Constant societal messages of female inferiority, which permeate institutions such as the family, education, and the mass media, are often accepted and reproduced by women even though they themselves are oppressed by this ideology.

Many of the narratives explored in this chapter exemplify how, to some degree, community members themselves accept negative ethnic and sexist stereotypes of Puerto Ricans. At the same time, however, and in spite of the pervasiveness and power of dominant group discourse, the Puerto Ricans presented here, and members of subordinate groups in general, are not passive recipients of these ideologies; they struggle against the internalization of inferiority, stereotyping, and prejudices and create positive self-images. Both processes are at work in the narratives analyzed in the following sections. Thus, the narratives of the Puerto Rican community in Brentwood reflect the internalization of and resistance to mainstream ideology about language, race and ethnicity, and gender.

Following Van Dijk's (1984, 1987) approach,[2] in the ensuing discussion, I examine various levels of discourse beginning, with such aspects of the global organization of talk as the topic of stories and the arguments provided by speakers to support their opinions. I also focus on local discourse features, for example semantic moves, which function to connect discourse propositions one to the next. These features include the use of strategies such as generalization, example, apparent concessions, repetition, contrast, mitigation, and displacement. I provide examples of each of these later. Conversational style and rhetoric are studied as well.

---

[2]Van Dijk (1984, 1987) argues that it is important to study the casual, informal talk about minorities by majority group members, because this discourse is one of the main vehicles for the reproduction of racism. He analyzes how majority group members speak about minority group persons in interviews conducted by majority group members. Through the study of individual texts, Van Dijk explores the social nature of racism.

Van Dijk (1984) argues that two principal aims characterize the discourse of the majority group: positive self-presentation and effective persuasion. When discussing sensitive topics such as minority communities, dominant group members are careful to present themselves as respectable, reasonable people, not as rabid racists. *Self-presentation* refers to the strategies people offer to present a positive image of themselves while simultaneously avoiding negative evaluations from interaction partners (Van Dijk, 1987). At the same time, dominant group members may hold prejudiced views about minority group members. They may wish to justify those opinions and to persuade the listener of their validity through the use of stories about minorities.

In minority discourse, positive self-presentation is complicated by internalized oppression because many community members have accepted or are struggling against dominant group representations of their community. This chapter makes explicit how internalized racism and sexism operate in Puerto Rican discourse and explores the strategies some speakers implement in order to challenge negative assessments of their ethnic or gender group.

THE POLITICS OF LANGUAGE

Language, which is integrally related to identity, has long been a source of both affirmation and discrimination to Latino/Latina populations in the United States. While language rights as an issue has served to unify diverse Latino/Latina groups throughout their political history in the United States (for example, around bilingual education and equal access in voting), some Latinos/Latinas contest the use of Spanish as a symbol of a specifically Latino/Latina identity (Flores & Yudice, 1990; Torres, 1990b). Next to race, language is the factor which most clearly serves to establish differences (Flores & Yudice, 1990) between Latinos and the dominant group. Those who argue that assimilation is the route Latino/Latinas should take in order to secure a better standard of living (Chavez, 1991) oppose others who argue for maintaining cultural distinctions, partly through language (Flores & Yudice, 1990).

The issue of Spanish versus English language use is central in the lives of the Puerto Ricans I interviewed. The first text I analyze in this chapter is a narrative by a second-generation, 40-year-old woman, in which she explains how she was motivated to learn English. The narrative was introduced in chapter 4 as Text 4-H (see pp. 83–84). Text 4-H is analyzed here in detail to examine the internalization of dominant group discourse.

At the level of form, this narrative has an orientation section from lines 2–9, followed by complicating actions interspersed with internal and external evaluations. In lines 22 and 23, there is another orientation sequence followed by more evaluation in lines 24–26 and finally an evaluation/resolution in line 27.

One striking aspect of this narrative, which suggests internalized oppression, is the identification of the problem and the blame meted out by the speaker. The context of the discussion is important. The narrator is explaining her views against bilingual education through a story about her own educational experiences. The story is occasioned by the desire to persuade the listener of her point of view; it is offered as a justification of her position against bilingual education. In the story, an Anglo child calls her a *spic* but she does not understand the insult, and the great shame of the misunderstanding compels her to learn English, without the aid of bilingual education. It seems that the speaker accepts the premise of the argument proposed, for example by proponents of the English Only movement, that in order to learn English, Latinos/Latinas just need to be more motivated. Many speakers, like the narrator of Text 4-H, use narratives of personal experience to justify their positions on controversial issues; they are considered strong evidence in support of the positions taken.

Evaluations are the place in the narrative where the narrator provides the most important information in the story; through a series of moves the narrator draws attention to the significance of the story being told. The participant who produced Text 4-H uses both internal and external evaluations in her story. Internal evaluative markers may occur at all levels: phonological, lexical, syntactic, and discourse levels (i.e., repetitions, reported speech, flashback, clustering around the peak of a story, etc.). External devices include commentary on the action of the story, generalizations drawn from a specific to a general case, and elaboration of information previously presented. Labov (1972) and Polanyi (1985) maintain that most narratives contain an evaluation of some sort that makes the point of the story clear and justifies why the narrator is telling the story in the first place. Linde (1993) points out that, in addition to establishing reportability, evaluations are used to demonstrate that the speaker shares the norms of the society and that she is a moral and good person. An analysis of evaluations also suggests those things that the speaker values and her understanding of how the world should function.

In this narrative, the speaker relies on internal evaluation to describe the events up to line 14; for example, the degree of the boy's insult is heightened by the use of intensifiers in line 6, *toda la vida* [all of my life]; also, the spitting noise rendered in line 13 and the expression of surprise offered in line 14 are examples of internal evaluation. These internal evaluations serve to dramatize her story and bring to life the emotions she felt at the time. Lines 16 through 18 offer an external evaluation; the listener learns the point of the narrative, or why the speaker finds it significant to tell. She explains through her story that the experience shamed her into learning English—so she learned English. The discourse marker *you know* in line 16, and the shift in the narrative to English, serve to draw to the attention of the listener that important information, in fact the point of the story, is coming. Lines 20–26 reiterate the point by offering a longer version of the same evaluation and a repetition of the insult. This section is interrupted by another orientation (lines 22–23) as the narrator remembers physical aspects of the boy in her story. She then concludes with more evaluation and a resolution.

Although the narrator describes the boy's racism, she does not condemn it. Instead, she castigates herself, as is clearly expressed in line 24. She describes her feelings of shame and humiliation at the time and, in retelling the story, again expresses these feelings. Her feelings toward the boy are not negative; she offers neutral, descriptive adjectives, as in lines 22 and 23. The narrative demonstrates her own feelings of inadequacy and how these feelings forced her to change her behavior quickly. The statement in line 19 that she forced herself to learn English is followed in line 20 by a concession introduced by the discourse coordinator *pero* [but]; that is, that Kevin showed her or taught her when he called her a *spic*. In line 26 the discourse marker *pero* serves to minimize or excuse the boy's behavior, because it motivated the narrator to learn English. She discovered that to avoid humiliation and shame she had to learn the language of the dominant group quickly. This in essence is the "moral" of the narrative; bilingual education is not necessary—instead, children with the "right" motivation will rapidly acquire English. The sentiment against bilingual education is not uncommon in the Brentwood Puerto Rican community.

Other stories about bilingualism and bilingual education, particularly in the first-generational data, similarly reproduce a primarily mainstream ideology about language and education. Another speaker, for example, tells a story about going to register her daughter in school and becoming furious when school officials tried to place her daughter in bilingual classes. The following text (Text 5-A) is part of her narrative:

Text 5-A

11) *y mi niña yo la puse en Manhattan*
12) *donde yo vivía*
13) *yo fui a registrarla*
14) *y se me subió la sangre*
15) *porque me dice la—*
16) *este, "Ana Rivera, programa bilingüe"*
17) *ay sin preguntarme*
18) *eh una cosa que cojen a la madre*
19) *que eh ignorante*
20) *entonce yo le dije,*

21) *"¿y por qué mi niña va pal programa bilingüe?"*
22) *"ay, porque ella eh hispana*
23) *y ella se beneficiará mucho*
24) *este con el programa bilingüe*
25) *y ella seguirá el idioma de su madre"*
26) *es, eh pura sicología*
27) *"pueh mira, la hija mía, eh fantástico, fantástico*
28) *pero la hija mía va pa clases regulares"*

[11) and my daughter I put her in Manhattan
12) where I was living
13) I went to register her
14) and my blood pressure went up
15) because the—says to me
16) well, "Ana Rivera, bilingual program"
17) oh without asking me
18) they assume that the mother
19) that she's ignorant
20) then I said to her,
21) "and why is my daughter going into a bilingual program?"
22) "Oh, because she is Hispanic
23) and she will benefit a lot
24) well with the bilingual program
25) and she will maintain her mother's language"
26) it is, it's pure psychology
27) "Well, look, my daughter, it's fantastic, fantastic
28) but my daughter is going into regular classes"]

In this sequence of Text 5-A, the mother makes her opposition to her daughter's participation in a bilingual education program clear. After a long orientation, she evaluates what is to follow in line 14. Then she uses reported speech, producing a dialogue between herself and a school official but interrupts it to evaluate the event externally in lines 17–19, remarking that school officials assume the ignorance of the parents and lure children into bilingual education. In lines 21–25 she cites the official's logic for placing the child in bilingual classes, namely that the child will benefit greatly and also maintain her mother's language. These justifications are dismissed as *pura sicología* [pure psychology] in line 26; this is another external evaluation that again interrupts the dialogue. In the last two lines of this sequence, lines 27–28, the narrator uses an internal evaluation strategy, sarcastically agreeing that bilingual education is *fantastic*, repeating this once in an exaggerated manner but stating that her daughter will be placed in mainstream classes. The narrative continues similarly for another 20 lines, with more reported speech and evaluations. The climax of the story occurs when the narrator informs the school official that she herself is working as a bilingual teacher and knows exactly what she wants and does not want for her daughter. The narrative emphatically expresses the speaker's negative feelings about bilingual education. As in the case of the first text, here a narrative of personal experience is occasioned by the desire of the narrator to justify her position on bilingual education.

In another narrative, a Puerto Rican speaker suggests that laws mandating English Only are necessary to motivate some Latinos to learn English. To explain his reasoning, the narrator essentially reproduces a dialogue (Text 5-B) between himself and an educated Dominican man who has been in the United States 20 years and has not learned English.

Text 5-B

1) *Hay personas que vienen*
2) *y caen en un sitio*
3) *que lo que se habla más*
4) *eh ehpañol*
5) *y no se preocupan*
6) *no se preocupan*
7) *yo, yo conohco un señor muy inteligente por cierto*
8) *él eh dominicano*
9) *él eh, según él velda?*
10) *yo creo*
11) *lo que él me dice*
12) *y él se ve*
13) *que eh una pelsona literada*
14) *en su país, según él, eh farmacéutico en su país*
15) *pero él lleva viviendo en este país, má de veinte años*
16) *y él no le habla ingléh*
17) *entonce yo estaba hablando con él*
18) *loh otro día, por cierto donde estaba cogiendo este curso*
19) *que él me hizo una invitación a su casa*
20) *y yo,*
21) *"ay peldona*
22) *no puedo il*
23) *polque ehte ehtoy cogiendo un culso en el colegio*
24) *y tengo que estudial"*
25) *y él me dijo,*
26) *"tú? tú estudiando?"*
27) *y yo le dije sí*
28) *dice,*
29) *"pero en español o en ingléh?"*

30) *"no, en inglé,*
31) *ay, no, no, no, no; no me digas*
32) *"tú no me digah eso, a mí no*
33) *yo con el ingléh no quiero nada"*
34) *y, y yo me solprendí*
35) *yo le dije,*
36) *"ay, pero como tú dice eso*
37) *un hombre que lleva viviendo aquí veinte año?"*
38) *"no, no, no, no, yo ehpañol sí*
39) *pero yo con el ingléh no quiero nada"*
40) *y entonce, yo le dije:*
41) *"pero mi'jo, ehtamoh en un paíh*
42) *que se habla inglé"*
43) *"a mí no me impolta*
44) *"a mí no me impolta"*
45) *yo le digo:*
46) *"pero que razón tú tiene para sentirte de esa manera"*
47) *y entonce me dice:*
48) *"es que yo creo*
49) *que nunca podré hablal el ingléh bien*
50) *y como nunca creo*
51) *que lo podré hablar inglés*
52) *pueh mejor no lo hablo*
53) *polque para que se burlen de mí*
54) *mejol no lo hablo"*
55) *pero esa eh una de la razoneh también*
56) *so en ese aspecto, eh que yo ehtaría de acueldo*

[1] There are people who come
2) and fall into a place
3) where what is spoken
4) is Spanish
5) and they aren't concerned
6) they aren't concerned
7) I, I know a man, very intelligent as a matter of fact
8) he is Dominican
9) he is, according to him, right
10) I believe
11) what he tells me
12) and you can see
13) that he is a literate person
14) in his country, according to him, he is a pharmacist in his country
15) but he has been living in this country, more than 20 years

16)   and he doesn't speak English
17)   so I was talking with him the other day
18)   as a matter of fact where I was taking this course
19)   that he invited me to his house
20)   and I,
21)   "Oh excuse me
22)   I can't go
23)   because I'm taking a course in college
24)   and I have to study"
25)   and he said to me,
26)   "You, you're studying?"
27)   and I said yes
28)   he said,
29)   "but in English or Spanish?"
30)   "No, in English"
31)   "Ohh, no, no, no, no, don't tell me
32)   you don't tell me that, no
33)   I don't want anything to do with English"
34)   and, and I was surprised
35)   I told him,
36)   "Oh, but how can you say that
37)   a man that has been living here 20 years"
38)   "no, no, no, no, me, Spanish, yes
39)   but I don't want anything to do with English"
40)   and then I told him,
41)   "but guy, we are in a country
42)   where English is spoken"
43)   "I don't care
44)   I don't care"
45)   and I said to him,
46)   "but what reason do you have to feel that way?"
47)   and then he said to me,
48)   "it's that I think
49)   that I will never be able to speak English well
50)   and because I don't think
51)   that I will be able to speak it English
52)   well I'd rather not speak it
53)   because if they are going to make fun of me
54)   I'd rather not speak it"
55)   but that is one of the reasons also
56)   so in that respect, is that I would agree]

This narrative was produced when I asked the speaker why he supported the English-only movement. In Text 5-B, the narrator, mainly through the use of reported speech, presents himself as someone seeking to better himself by taking classes in English. He implicitly contrasts himself with his interlocutor who claims that he does not want to learn English because he believes that he will never speak it well, and others might make fun of him. Through a strategy of repetition (lines 30–32, 38, 43–44) the narrator highlights his friend's extreme resistance toward learning English. Not only does the narrative serve to justify the speaker's approval of English-only legislature, he simultaneously shows himself to be a "good" U.S. citizen, while implicitly criticizing the other man through a strategy of contrast. Although the other man is said to be an educated, intelligent person (lines 7, 13–14), this presentation is undermined by the fact that he refuses to learn English. In the resolution-coda of the narrative (lines 55–56), the narrator ends by stating that English-only laws exist because of people like his friend and he agrees with such laws. Like this narrator, those members of the Brentwood community who support English-only laws have internalized the untrue premise that most Latinos refuse to learn English.

The theme of language and the mixed feelings that it evokes often emerges in the data, especially in the stories and conversations of Groups 1 and 2. The narratives reveal insecurity around language issues, the internalization of negative evaluations of Spanish, as well as a lack of criticism toward discriminatory practices in the United States. Although in other places in their conversations all of the narrators I quote here claim that it is important for the community to maintain Spanish language and culture, they all produce narratives that seem to accept mainstream ideology concerning a public and private split between English and Spanish. As dominant discourse dictates, English is valued as the language of success and advancement, whereas Spanish is associated with emotional, private spheres (see survey results, chap. 1). The narrators, especially in their evaluations, attempt to present themselves as moral and good U.S. citizens; they value the dominant language and see the schools as a public sphere where only English is legitimate. They have internalized mainstream norms about the English language and, moreover, they show that they are ready to criticize those who do not share these norms, as does the narrator in Text 5-B.

THE PRESENTATION OF ETHNIC IDENTITY

The contradiction between affirming Latino culture and identity on the one hand and subscribing to racist and ethnocentric ideologies on the other is not only present in discourse about language. Other narratives exemplify the contradictory attitudes and feelings community members have toward their ingroup, and specifically the internalization of dominant group stereotypes. In one narrative (Text 5-C), a 40-year-old Group 2 man tells a story about seeking to rent an apartment.

Text 5-C

1) *me mudé con la ayuda de mi secretaría*
2) *llamó a un sitio*
3) *y habló con un señor judío*
4) *donde yo vivo el señor es judío*
5) *ella es mexicana*
6) *él trabaja en la ciudad*
7) *y ella trabajaba allá*
8) *le dijo,*
9) *"el jefe está divorciado*
10) *y está, está buscando apartamento*
11) *pero él está buscando en el* Penny Saver"
12) *y dice,*
13) *"pero yo quiero mejol para él*
14) *no una porquería*
15) *poque él no tiene vicios,*
16) *no bebe"*
17) *bueno entonces yo fui yo fui a ver el apartamento*
18) *y él me dice a mí:*
19) *"por aquí to todo el mundo es es blanquito*
20) *mira la persona anteriormente tenía problemas*
21) *porque era un prieto"*
22) *y tenía miedo*
23) *y allí me di cuenta*
24) *que poque era puertorriqueño*
25) *le estaba metiendo miedo*
26) *"mira le voy a decir sinceramente*
27) *yo soy un puertorriqueño criado aquí en Nueva York* ok
28) *me crié en el tiempo que estaba la guerra del* Vietnam
29) *me crié en los tiempos de—*
30) *yo yo he visto*
31) I've seen years of all different generations, 1950s, 60s, 70s and the 80s
32) *todos todos diferentes*
33) *desde luego cada uno ha sido diferente*
34) *no uso droga*
35) *no fumo*
36) *no tengo vicio*
37) *me divorcié*
38) *poque como tampoco es algo malo*
39) *trabajo con una agencia ayudando a la gente*
40) *estoy buscando un sitio para estabilizarme* oh ok"
41) *le dije,*

42)   "well *usted me avisa*"
43)   *entonces como a la una de la tarde o a la una y media regresé*
       aquí
44)   *y la llamada que quería darme el apartamento*
45)   *o sea para noviembre*
46)   *y dice,*
47)   *"¿para cuándo quiere usted mudar?"*
48)   *yo, "no, no, pa principios del mes de diciembre"*
49)   *y "no no no si quieres múdate ahora"*
50)   *"oh boy primero que no tengo muebles*
51)   *no tengo . . ."*
52)   *"no" dice,*
53)   *"yo te empresto"*
54)   *me dice,*
55)   *quería prestarme una cama que si esto*
56)   *pues yo le dije,*
57)   *"yo soy una persona*
58)   *que no tiene vicios*
59)   *mujeres entrando en mi casa*
60)   *no la va a ver*
61)   *polque no acostumbro a estar así*
62)   *no soy un hombre mujeriego*
63)   *que va a estar siempre entrando*
64)   *nunca estoy ahí"*
65)   *y es verdad que yo salgo de mi trabajo*
66)   *voy a mi casa*
67)   *me cambio de ropa*
68)   *me voy a andal*
69)   *a veces llego a las once de la noche a dormil,* ok
70)   *tengo una amiga*
71)   *que va a la casa*
72)   *ella siempre sale*
73)   *tampoco se queda allí*
74)   *"pero si tú tienes una persona amiga*
75)   *que se quiera quedal*
76)   *y vivir contigo*
77)   *te vale cien dólares"*
78)   *que, que digo la renta más*
79)   *ya, ya sabe*
80)   *que me tiene que poner*
81)   *le dije,*
82)   *"que no, que pol eso no va a tener ningún problema"*
83)   *y este nunca, me paso en las casa*

84)   *él me oye*
85)   *cuando llego*
86)   *el perro sabe avisar*
87)   *cuando yo llego*
88)   *poque un perro que el perro ladra*
89)   *y yo abro mi puerta por la mañana*
90)   *me voy a dormir*
91)   *y no lo veo*
92)   *hoy lo veo*
93)   *poque tengo que pagal la renta*
94)   y de allí no lo veo más

[1]   I moved with the help of my secretary
2)   she called a place
3)   and talked with a Jewish man
4)   where I live the man is Jewish
5)   she is Mexican
6)   he works in the city
7)   and she was working there
8)   she said to him,
9)   "the boss is divorced
10) and is, is looking for an apartment
11) but he is looking in the Penny Saver"
12) and she says,
13) "but I want better for him
14) not a filthy place
15) because he doesn't have bad habits,
16) he doesn't drink"
17) well then I went I went to see the apartment
18) and he tells me,
19) "around here everyone is is White
20) look the last person had problems
21) because he was Black"
22) and he was afraid
23) and then I realized   ·
24) that because I was Puerto Rican
25) I was scaring him
26) "look I'm going to tell you sincerely
27) I am a Puerto Rican raised here in New York ok
28) I was raised during the time of the Vietnam War
29) I was raised in the times of—
30) I I have seen
31) I've seen years of all different generations, 1950s, 60s, 70s, and
      the 80s

32)   all all different
33)   from then each one has been different
34)   I don't use drugs
35)   I don't smoke
36)   I don't have bad habits
37)   I divorced
38)   because it's also not something bad
39)   I work with an agency helping people
40)   I am looking for a place to establish myself oh ok"
41)   I said to him,
42)   "well you let me know me"
43)   then around one in the afternoon or 1:30 I returned here
44)   and the call that he wanted to give me the apartment
45)   in other words for November
46)   and he says,
47)   "when do you want to move?"
48)   I: "no, no, for the beginning of the month of December"
49)   and "no no no if you want move now"
50)   "oh boy first I don't have furniture
51)   I don't have"
52)   "no" he says
53)   "I'll loan you"
54)   he says to me
55)   he wanted to lend me a bed
56)   well I said to him,
57)   "I am a person
58)   that does not have bad habits
59)   women coming to my house
60)   you're not going to see it
61)   because I'm not accustomed to being like that
62)   I am not a ladies' man
63)   that's going to always be entering
64)   I am never here"
65)   and it's true that I leave my work
66)   I go home
67)   I change clothes
68)   I go walking
69)   sometimes I arrive at eleven at night to sleep, ok
70)   I have a female friend
71)   that goes to the house
72)   she always leaves
73)   she doesn't stay there
74)   "but if you have a person a female friend

75)   that wants to stay
76)   and to live with you
77)   it will cost you one hundred dollars"
78)   that, that I mean more rent
79)   you already know
80)   that you have to put
81)   I said to him
82)   no, because you're not going to have any problem
83)   and I'm never at home
84)   he hears me
85)   when I arrive
86)   the dog knows how to warn
87)   when I arrive
88)   because a dog that the dog barks
89)   and I open my door in the morning
90)   I go to sleep
91)   and I don't see him
92)   today I see him
93)   because I have to pay the rent
94)   and from there I don't see him anymore]

Nowhere in this story is the narrator critical of the Anglo landlord who was reluctant to rent him an apartment because he is Puerto Rican. In fact, in the majority of the long narrative he lists the virtues he has that he hopes will differentiate him from other Puerto Ricans. He does not directly set himself apart in the narrative, but immediately afterwards, in the course of my conversation with him, he offers the following sequence (Text 5-D):

Text 5-D

1)   *Pero este nosotros mismos hemos dado la mala reputación*
2)   *yo siempre lo he dicho*
3)   *hemos dado una reputación*
4)   *porque vamos a los sitios*
5)   *en vez de comportarnos como gente, esto es en términos general*
6)   *nos comportamos como animales*
7)   *¿cuántos apartamentos destruimos?*
8)   *claro la experiencia siempre* catches up to you

[1)   But, well, we have given ourselves the bad reputation
2)   I have always said it
3)   we have given a reputation
4)   because we are going to the places
5)   instead of behaving like people, this is in general terms

6)   we behave like animals
7)   how many apartments do we destroy
8)   of course the experience always catches up to you]

In lines 1 through 8 in Text 5-D, the narrator remarks that Puerto Ricans are destructive and are to blame for their bad reputation. In line 6, he uses a simile to compare Puerto Ricans to animals, although he mitigates the statement somewhat in line 5 with "esto es en términos general" ["this is in general terms"]. However, he reinforces the statement in line 7 with the rhetorical question: "¿Cuántos apartamentos destruimos?" ["How many apartments do we destroy?"], which is also an appeal to the listener, because the narrator assumes that it is shared knowledge that Puerto Ricans destroy apartments. This narrator both identifies with the Puerto Rican community and sets himself apart from it. Thus, he uses the first person plural verb form, *nosotros*, when describing the damage Puerto Ricans do, but only after spending 94 lines in a narrative (Text 5-C) explaining how he, as an individual, is different from other Puerto Ricans and can be trusted to be a model renter. In this regard, the mitigation in line 5 probably also serves to distinguish him from the other Puerto Ricans.

Taking all of his texts as a whole, we can see that this narrator uses several strategies to establish himself as different from the rest of his community. These include direct and indirect reported speech, and repetition. Tannen (1989) argues that these are involvement strategies that speakers use to heighten their listeners' interest in the unfolding story. In Text 5-D, direct speech and repetition apparently serve as strategies to persuade the listener that the narrator is a good and moral person in direct contrast to his community. In lines 13 to 16, the narrator directly quotes his secretary who lists his virtues. He presents a longer list of his good qualities in lines 27 to 40. Here the narrator offers direct speech again, this time in the guise of his remarks to the landlord, when he recognizes that the landlord is hesitant to rent him an apartment. He repeats some of the good qualities mentioned by his secretary: He does not drink, smoke, or take drugs; and he adds new qualities, such as his maturity and work for a social service agency. In lines 57 to 64 again the narrator repeats in direct speech what he told the landlord about his good virtues. Then the narrator continues with a list of his other good qualities.

Whether the quoted words were ever uttered is unimportant. Tannen (1989) points out that dialogue in conversation, as in literature, is a creative act that the storyteller uses to ensure listener involvement. The dramatization of dialogue is also a strategy that allows the narrator to repeat whatever he wants to emphasize. In this narrative, for instance, the speaker wants to highlight his positive characteristics. He does this internally at least twice, through the use of another speaker's (his secretary's) reported speech and his own reported dialogue with the landlord. Then he continues to evaluate himself externally by listing his daily activities in the rest of the narrative, contrasting himself implicitly to stereotypes of Puerto Ricans that he himself has internalized.

The contradictory struggle over the meaning of *Puerto Rican identity* in the stories is most interesting when conflicting ideologies co-occur in the same narrative as opposed to in different stories or comments. For example, another participant, a 37 year old (Group 2), woman, offers the following story, Text 5-E, as a part of a series of narratives on the immigration of her family to the city:

Text 5-E

1) *yo sí sé que cuando yo me mudé a Nueva York*
2) *mi mamá era la primera familia hispana en ese en ese sitio*
3) *y ese sitio era bello*
4) *y después a los diez años estaba destruido*
5) *y yo me acuerdo de eso*
6) *so puede ser . . .*
7) you see it Lourdes, What can I tell you?, *ja ja ja*
8) *mira cuando yo me mudé allá yo tenía cinco años*
9) *el sitio era de los mas bellos*
10) *era east, era, este,* Fulton Street of South Bronx
11) *mi mamá, mi mamá que me crió es morena de Loisaida*
12) *y ella fue la primera familia que se mudó*
13) *y ese sitio era bello*
14) *y en quince años después ese sitio está ese sitio ya no existe*

I: *¿y cómo te explicas tú eso?*

15) *bueno yo no sé*
16) *pero yo veía los americanos yéndose y los hispanos viniendo*
17) *. . . so como, como nina jóven que yo voy a decir?*
18) *sin embargo yo sí sé*
19) *que toda mi vida yo voy a trabajar con niños hispanos*

[1) I do know that when I moved to New York
2) my mother was the first Hispanic family in that, in that area
3) and that place was beautiful
4) and then ten years later it was destroyed
5) and I remember that
6) so it could be—
7) you see it Lourdes, What can I tell you?, ha ha ha
8) Look, when I moved there
9) I was five years old and the place was beautiful

10)   it was east, it was umm Fulton Street of the South Bronx
11)   My mother, my mother who raised is Black from Loisaida
12)   and she was the first family that moved there
13)   and the place was beautiful
14)   and fifteen years later that place is, that place doesn't exist

I: And how do you explain that?

15)   well I don't know
16)   but I would see the Americans leaving and the Hispanics
       arriving
17)   . . . so as, as a young girl what am I going to say?
18)   and in spite of that I do know
19)   that all of my life I am going to work with Hispanic children]

In Text 5-E, the narrator explains how her neighborhood deteriorated
when Latinos moved in. She seems at some level, to have internalized
the racist American ideology about minority people being dirty and
destructive that we also saw expressed in the previous story (Text 5-D).
Yet, unlike the previous narrator, she both resists this ideology and
appears to have assimilated it. She does not wish to disassociate herself
from her community and is concerned with her self-presentation as a
Puerto Rican woman before an ingroup interlocutor. Thus, she does not
state negative information directly but expresses her views rather
indirectly through a series of semantic, stylistic, and rhetorical moves
(Van Dijk 1984, 1987), including contrast, rhetorical questions, repetition, denial, understatement, displacement and mitigation. Each of
these is described in the next paragraph.
    The speaker never explicitly states that she feels Latino/Latinas
destroyed the neighborhood but leads the listener to this conclusion
through a series of moves. First, she sets up a contrast in lines 3 and 4
for the listener to draw her own conclusions. Line 6 begins with the
English discourse marker *so,* which may function to indicate that a
conclusion, that has been motivated in the preceding units, is to follow
(Schiffrin, 1987). However, the speaker hesitates and never completes
the thought. In line 7, she switches to English, addresses the interviewer
with a rhetorical question, and laughs. These three features indicate
that she recognizes that her assessment might be problematic for me as
an ingroup member interlocutor.
    Next the speaker proceeds to substantiate her argument, again
indirectly. She repeats the original contrast, except now with more
details (lines 10–14). When encouraged by the interviewer to state her
assessment directly, she relies on the move of ignorance or denial (as
defined by Van Dijk, 1985). In line 15 she says *"bueno yo no sé"* ["well I

don't know"], and in line 16, again, indirectly states the situation without evaluating it. In line 17, the discourse marker *so* again suggests that a conclusion is to follow that is warranted by the offered information or by general knowledge of the situation. But rather than offer a direct conclusion the narrator relies on the strategy of displacement—it is not she as an adult who makes the point, but the perspective coming from herself as a little girl. Linde (1993) refers to this strategy as a property of reflexivity. This strategy allows the speaker to distance herself from the protagonist in the narrative. In the narrative, the speaker can function as one self among many selves and can create distance between a past self and a more recent self, in order to rationalize or excuse the actions of the protagonist—as in this example.

In line 17, she appeals to me as the interlocutor with another rhetorical question that again avoids directly responding to the issue. Nevertheless, although never directly stated, the speaker's point comes across clearly. Indirectly acknowledging that she has offered a negative assessment of her community, she mitigates the harshness of the statement in lines 18 and 19 by stating that, in spite of this situation, her life's work will always be directed toward the care of Latino children.

That some Puerto Rican speakers in Brentwood accept the stereotype of Latinos as destructive is not surprising given the saturation of racist ideology across U.S. culture. Fanon (1967) argues that racist messages are a constant and insidious part of society present in schools, books, newspapers, advertisements, films, and radio programs. The racist propositions become part of the consciousness of both dominant and minority group members. Racial and ethnic groups living in the same context as the dominant group, exposed to the same ideology, may come to accept some aspects of the dominant group viewpoint, even when it casts minority group members in a negative light. At the same time that minority group members reject racist ideology, they still assimilate it to some degree. As Matsuda (1993) states:

> At some level, no matter how much both victims and well meaning dominant-group members resist it, racial inferiority is planted in our minds as an idea that may hold some truth. The idea is improbable and abhorrent, but because it is presented repeatedly, it is there before us. "Those people," are lazy, dirty, sexualized, money grubbing, dishonest, inscrutable, we are told. We reject the idea, but the next time we sit next to one of "those people" the dirt message, the sex message is triggered. We stifle it, reject it as wrong, but it is there, interfering with our perception and interaction with the person next to us. (pp. 25–26)

However, as is evident by the narrator's hesitation and discomfort in Text 5-E, Brentwood Puerto Ricans do not simply adopt the dominant group ideology, and are often quite ambivalent about the conclusions they themselves are drawing. One conscious or subconscious response might be to disassociate one's self from the minority group; another might be to fight against the internalization of such discourse. As we have seen, both solutions are found in the narratives and in the community in general.

Participants from Group 3, the youngest group, tend to speak more overtly about racial and ethnic discrimination and to reject racist dominant group discourse. In contrast with the foregoing narratives produced by Group 1 and 2 speakers, when the younger generation discusses discrimination, they directly name and critique it. A narrative (Text 5-F) by a younger community member tells how she was refused a job because she is Puerto Rican. She explains that she took the case to court, won, got the job, and became a much-trusted employee. The following evaluation and resolution of the narrative are her comments about the employer:

Text 5-F

31) *así eh para que ella aprenda*
32) *que sólo porque uno eh puertorriqueño . . .*
33) *no quiere decir*
34) *que uno no puede tener confianza con un puertorriqueño*
35) because *a veceh, nosotros somos mejores*
36) *que la misma clase de elloh*
37) that's the truth.

[31) so uh so that she understands
32) that just because one is Puerto Rican . . .
33) does not mean
34) that one cannot have confidence in a Puerto Rican
35) because sometimes, we are better
36) than the same class of them
37) that's the truth.]

From a personal narrative where she uses the first person singular throughout, the narrator shifts to the first person plural in the final evaluation (line 35) where she generalizes from her individual experience to that of the Puerto Rican community. This is in contrast to the male narrator of Text 5-D who uses his personal example to distinguish himself from the community. The young narrator here in Text 5-F uses her personal example to show that Puerto Ricans are sometimes more trustworthy than Anglos. She thus resists the internalization of racist messages about her community.

GENDERED VOICES

Discussion of gender relations in the community occasioned the telling of many narratives, especially among the women. This is not to suggest that men do not also produce narratives on this topic (Torres, 1992b), but men were not as forthcoming with such narratives, probably, in part, because the interviewer was a woman.[3]

In the narratives of Group 1 and Group 2 speakers, there is little verbal critique of patriarchal gender arrangements, although often stories that are not externally evaluated contradict these relations. The women from Groups 1 and 2 do not seem to have a language to explicitly express rebellion against the status quo. In the following narrative (Text 5-G) about growing up with a violent father, for example, a 50-year-old Group 1 woman tells about the time her father picked up her little sister and threatened to hit her against the wall; the father threw the narrator out of the house when she tried to defend her sister.

Text 5-G

1) *y un día me botó de la casa*
2) *porque cogió a mi hermana*
3) *en el Bronx, sí*
4) *me me cogió*
5) *y y cogió mi hermana pequeña para darle en contra la pared*
6) *porque él era así*
7) *entonces yo me paré para quitársela*
8) *mamá no se atrevía*
9) *pero yo me atreví*
10) *y y bendito para que fue eso*
11) *cuando yo "mira deje esa muchacha quieta*
12) *como Ud. le va a dar con la pared?"*
13) *y vino y me la soltó*
14) *y la puso en el piso*
15) *y me ha dao un arevé a mí por aquí encima*
16) *que me dejó loca*
17) *y me dijo,*
18) *"y ahora te me largas de aquí ahora mismo"*
19) *y cogí y me salí al jol*
20) *y mamá dijo,*
21) *"Usted no se va*

---

[3]Silberstein (1988), in a study of male and female courtship narratives, finds differences in gender related narrative devices. Riessman (1988) finds differences of style in the narratives of Puerto Rican and Anglo women; she also (1987) discusses the problems persons from outside ethnic or racial communities may have in interpreting narratives in an article appropriately titled "When gender is not enough."

22)   *el que se va eh él*
23)   *entre pa dentro es él que se va"*
24)   *y él dijo,*
25)   *"yo no me voy"*
26)   *lo que pasó, después se puso a pensal*
27)   *y entonces fue cuando se fue pa Puerto Rico, ¿te acuerdas?*
28)   *y dijo que entre mamá y yo le le habían dao le habíamos dao en la cara*

[1)   And one day he threw me out of the house
2)   because he took my sister
3)   in the Bronx, yeah
4)   he took me
5)   and and he took my younger sister to hit her into, against the wall
6)   because he was like that
7)   then I got up to take her away from him
8)   mama didn't dare
9)   but I dared
10) and and god what was that for
11) when, I "look (formal) leave that girl alone
12) how can you (formal) hit her against the wall?"
13) and he went and let her go
14) and he put her on the floor
15) and he gave me a punch, over here (points to her head)
16) that left me crazy
17) and he told me,
18) "and now get the hell out of here right now"
19) and I took and I went out into the hall
20) and mama said,
21) "You (formal) are not going
22) the one that's leaving is him
23) come in here he is the one that's leaving"
24) and he said,
25) "I'm not leaving"
26) what happened, later he got to thinking
27) then it was that he left for Puerto Rico, remember?
28) and he said that between my mother and me we had hit, we had hit him in the face]

The narrator does not directly critique her father's violence. The only understated external evaluation offered about his actions is in line 6, the statement that he did these things *"porque él era así"* ["because he was like that"].

Although the narratives of the younger women in Group 3 reveal an internalization of values that have traditionally been associated with Puerto Rican women (Alvarez, 1988), including an unquestioned respect for the authority of males (specifically fathers and husbands), they also contradict the stereotype of the passive Latina. This is not to say that resistance is absent from the narratives of first generation women. In the narrative just mentioned (Text 5-G), the women in the house do join together and eventually throw the father out of the house. An important difference, however, is that younger narrators frequently externally evaluate sexist situations through the use of explicit verbal analyses of the problem, whereas the older women are less likely to directly name and critique male oppression. Thus, younger women have claimed an explicit language that confronts male power. For example, in the language use survey, it was women from Group 3 who mention sexism as a form of discrimination that Latinas suffer (see chap. 2).

In the following section of a Group 3 narrative (Text 5-H), a 19-year-old woman talks about a friend who is being battered by her boyfriend. According to the narrator, not only does she advise her friend to call the police when she is abused, she also confronts him directly. In the following portion of the narrative, she talks about her response to the situation:

Text 5-H

13) *yo hablo con él*
14) *él eh mi amigo*
15) *pero yo se lo digo en la cara a él también*
16) if I have to
17) because I've told him before
18) I think he's wrong
19) *él no tiene ningún derecho pa coger*
20) *y caerle encima a ella*
21) *ella no eh su hija*
22) *él dice*
23) *"ay eso eh*
24) *porque ella eh tremenda* bitch"
25) *así me dice,*
26) "no," I go
27) *"eso no eh razón*
28) *eso no eh razón"*

[13] I talk with him
14) he is my friend
15) but I tell him also right to his face

16)   if I have to
17)   because I've told him before
18)   I think he's wrong
19)   he has no right to take her
20)   and beat her up
21)   she's not his daughter
22)   he says,
23)   "oh, that it's
24)   because she is a tremendous bitch"
25)   that's what he tells me
26)   "no," I go
27)   "that's not a reason
28)   that's not a reason"]

However, in this narrative we again see contradictory messages about gender norms, which suggest an ongoing struggle to define Latina women's status. On the one hand, there is a very explicit condemnation of the boyfriend's behavior throughout the narrative section. She repeats her condemnation several times (lines 17–21, 26–28); she reports that she confronted the boyfriend and challenged him directly. On the other hand, line 21 ["she's not his daughter"], suggests that there are possibly legitimate reasons for a male to beat a female. The narrator couches the situation in terms of rights and determines that although boyfriends do not have the right to beat their girlfriends, fathers do have the right to beat their daughters. This struggle for the meaning of Puerto Rican women's identity is present in many Group 3 narratives.

The contradiction between acceptance of sexist gender roles and resistance to them is also at work in the narrative introduced in chapter 4 as Text 4-I (see pages 86–87). The story was produced by an 18-year-old woman who was born and raised in the Brentwood community. She is a teacher in a Head Start Program. The narrative was occasioned by a discussion during the interview on the subjects the woman taught the children. Among other things, she states that she spoke to them about how to protect themselves from sexual abuse. She uses a narrative of personal experience to support her decision to warn children to denounce abusive adults.

In this story the narrator describes a time when her uncle attempted to sexually abuse her. She directly confronts the abuser and tells her mother of the incident. The narrative has the usual structure of a narrative of personal experience. It has a long orientation section, from lines 1 to 12, followed by an evaluation section from 13 to 16. The complicating actions from lines 17 to 20 are followed by more evaluation, and a section from line 23 to line 29 in which the speaker reproduces an entire monologue she directed to the abuser. This is followed by another evaluation section, lines 30 to 33, a coda and resolution, lines 33–34.

Whereas the narrator explains the incident in a very direct and forthright manner, it is interesting to observe the vague language used to express the attempted molestation, which is never named directly. Instead, the narrator uses euphemisms as in line 5, "take advantage of," line 13, *"tratar de ponerse fresco"* ["try to get fresh"], lines 16, 23, and 26, *"hacer una cosa así"* ["do something like that"]. Yet, later, when referring to the harasser, the narrator loses all timidity and states rather directly in line 29 that she asked him, *"¿Qué tú no puedes ir por allá a encontrar crica?"* ["What can't you go out and get some pussy"]. All indirectness is lost and the issue becomes one of embarrassing the uncle as an inadequate man because he cannot get sex out on the street, but rather has to solicit sex from a young family member. She can be more explicit here, perhaps because he, rather than she, is now the focus of attention and also because she is venting her anger.

The narrative is heavily evaluated both internally (line 3 and in the direct quote from lines 22–29) and especially externally (lines 2, 6, 13–15, 19, 30–34). It is in these evaluations that the narrator expresses her interpretation of the incident. In this narration, particularly in the evaluations, we see elements of what Ruskin and Varenne (1983) describe as typical of Puerto Rican discourse on conflict. Criticism is framed not as a violation of the narrator's individual rights, but rather, as in this case, as the uncle's betrayal of his role as a family member.

This story suggests that the narrator has internalized traditional Latino/Latina values about family roles and male behavior. Although the married uncle is critiqued for violating his role as uncle, it is understood that he has the right to sex (line 29); the problem is simply that he was looking for it within the family rather than elsewhere. However, the narrative also offers a strong repudiation of the passive roles usually assigned to women in Latino/Latina culture. This is evidenced by the narrator's direct speech, which presents her fighting back and forcefully confronting her uncle verbally, as well as by her determination to teach children to protect themselves. This narrative demonstrates how the meaning of Puerto Rican womanhood is being struggled over in one community member's discourse. In the narrative, a contradictory dichotomy is present; both traditional values and values challenging those traditions co-occur in the same narrative.

The presentation of gender identity in the narratives, then, is never clear cut and unambiguous. An analysis of both content and discourse features and strategies reveals how Puerto Rican women in Brentwood attempt to integrate traditional role expectations with perceptions and actions that challenge these understandings.

CONCLUSION

In this chapter, linguistic and interpretive approaches are utilized to examine gender role negotiation and the reproduction of internalized oppression in the discourse of Puerto Ricans living in Brentwood. The analysis represents an effort to examine how speakers reveal their social ideology and perception of self through topic choice, development of positions, and manipulation of linguistic strategies. Dominant group "stories" or schemas pervade the narratives of the Puerto Rican speakers in my data. Three dominant group schemas discussed are: (a) Education should be in the majority language; (b) minority group persons are destructive and the cause of decay in the neighborhood; and (c) men have an inalienable right to sex and violence. The first two schemas represent topics that are very common in racist discourse. Van Dijk (1987) finds that there is a set of prejudiced semantic macrostructures that are frequent in the talk of majority group members concerning "foreigners" in both Amsterdam and San Diego. Racist stories can be summarized and categorized according to their underlying semantic macrostructure. The topics that are produced are predictability found in racist talk about whatever group is considered "foreign" in a given context. In the Puerto Rican discourse analyzed here, the various realizations of comparable semantic macrostructures may be viewed as manifestations of internalized racism in the Brentwood community. Similarly, the production of stories that can be subsumed under the third semantic macrostructure suggests that Puerto Ricans in Brentwood have internalized sexism.

In the discourse of Puerto Rican men and women, such schemata are resisted at times in the same or a different text by the same (or another) speaker from the community. Often these schemata are not unproblematically accepted and reproduced in the discourse of speakers; rather, they are challenged both at the level of content and through the use of linguistic and discourse strategies. The contradictory positions Puerto Ricans experience in the context of a racist and sexist society are continually being worked out in discourse. As we have seen, an ongoing struggle for social identity and meaning is evident in the narratives and thus in the Brentwood community at large. Often discourses of the dominant culture and of subordinate cultures confront each other in the same narratives; and thus in the narratives, status quo racial and gender relations are dynamically reproduced and resisted.

6

Conclusion

I locate the general conclusions gleaned from my study of three groups of Puerto Rican speakers in the United States in the context of societal and individual differences of language evolution. My ethnographic study and the language use survey I administered indicate that Spanish is a language of restricted use for Puerto Rican young people. The vast majority of Puerto Rican participants, born and raised in New York, have learned Spanish at home and most have never been formally educated in the language. Spanish is an oral language. Compared to their parents, and even young people of different Latino nationalities, Puerto Rican young people in Brentwood are using Spanish less, with fewer speakers, and under restricted contexts, such as with monolingual relatives or with parents who continue to speak Spanish to their children. The young people say that Spanish is important to them; they express much loyalty to the language and wish to continue using it. However, the associations made with Spanish are primarily affective rather than instrumental. For most young people, knowledge of Spanish is not deemed essential for a Latino identity; although they all identify strongly as Puerto Rican, language is not the sole or major ingredient of that identity.

An examination of structural issues (narrative components and the verbal tenses associated with each, overall Spanish verb use, and clause complexity), however, reveals little evidence of the simplification and loss across generations found in other studies. English-dominant Puerto Ricans are able narrators demonstrating a wide variety of storytelling skills. The structure of their narratives is as complete and rich as the narratives of older, seemingly more proficient Spanish speakers. They use verb inflections appropriate to the grammatical context and to the narrative components of their stories. In a few cases, such as with conditionals, change across generations is evident; but much variation with regard to this structure exists in the speech of the Spanish monolingual group also. With regard to syntactic complexity, or the use of coordination and subordination in the clause construction, there is also little difference across groups. English-dominant speakers utilize a range of nominal, adjectival, and adverbial structures in their oral narratives comparable to that of Spanish-dominant speakers.

117

Not unexpectedly, the greatest differences in the Spanish speech of the three groups studied here occur at the lexical level. The English-dominant group uses many more English borrowings than the other two groups when speaking Spanish. However, the type of loanword borrowing that they favor is noteworthy. Many times they resort to a strategy of calquing, whereby words already in the Spanish language acquire a new meaning from the lending language. This type of borrowing arguably preserves the integrity of the Spanish language more so than other types of borrowing and involves innovative uses of Spanish. The young Puerto Ricans who are English-dominant also engage in code-mixing much more frequently than do Spanish-dominant speakers. They resort to the strategy of code-mixing to enhance, rather than replace, many of the narrative strategies employed by the Spanish-dominant and bilingual groups. The most surprising finding with regard to the incorporation of English in the Spanish discourse of the English-dominant speakers, however, is the low frequency of English use overall. The results of this study suggest that the perception by community members and some linguists that the Spanish of U.S. Latinos is marked by frequent use of English is inaccurate. As I have shown, English single-word borrowings account for only 1.9% of the total word output of all of the narratives. Mixing at the clause level is 3 times greater for English-dominant speakers than Spanish-dominant speakers; but this accounts for less than 10% of all their utterances above the word level. Obviously the young Puerto Ricans, born and raised in the U.S., use English in their narratives much more than the other two groups, but I would argue that this is a very low frequency for speakers who are otherwise more comfortable speaking English.

I also explored the content of the oral narratives of personal experience. Too often in studies on U.S. Spanish, sociolinguists ignore the words of the community; we tend to focus on the grammatical aspects of language use and rarely on the message conveyed. I looked at the narratives as constructions of gendered and ethnically marked identities. I analyzed stories that demonstrate the very difficult position in which Puerto Ricans find themselves in the United States. The speakers generate discourses of both the dominant and oppressed cultures in their narratives. In examining the actual content of the narratives, I found that all speakers, to a greater or lesser extent, have internalized dominant ideologies of gender, ethnicity, and language, at the same time that they struggle against such discourse. Young and old alike are contending with issues of internalized racism and sexism, and they use similar strategies to work through these issues. One difference noted in the narratives is that the younger community members tend to be more explicit than older generation speakers in their challenges to dominant paradigms. This analysis of the discourse of the community reveals how the status quo is both reproduced and resisted in the narratives and how ideological forces work with other factors, such as attitudes, to influence the choices speakers make concerning language use.

It would be disingenuous to argue that the Spanish spoken by second, third, and succeeding generations is unaffected by a context of restricted input and use. This is not my intention. As the LPTF (1978) states, "it is necessary to be both critical and politically astute to recognize that whereas the structure of a language may evolve over centuries and be indifferent to loans and interference, the sociolinguistic patterns and use of language can and have been changed in a few generations both for good and ill" (p. 28). This statement cogently reflects the findings of the present research. There is a shift in the overall use of Spanish by Puerto Rican young people compared to their parents. They speak Spanish in fewer contexts and with less people than earlier generations. English-dominant speakers use more English borrowings and code-mix more than Spanish-dominant and bilingual speakers. But few differences are registered with regard to the verb structure and clause construction of the home language. And all Puerto Ricans in my study generate powerful, complex narratives about themselves and their lives in the community.

IMPLICATIONS OF SOCIOLINGUISTIC RESEARCH

The implications of this work concern the study of language maintenance and shift, the analysis of structural features of the language, and the study of Spanish in the United States in general. When we analyze language maintenance and shift in any community, we must keep in mind the specific geographic, political, and social context. In the case of Brentwood, we are describing a community near New York City, which, like the metropolitan area, is immersed in Latino culture and continues to attract many Latinos through immigration. Puerto Ricans were the original Latino subgroup to populate Brentwood, and they are still the dominant Latino group, although the recent influx of immigrants is primarily Central American. Contact between old and new immigrant groups is fraught with tension, but Latino community groups are working to help the new immigrants get acclimated. The influx has revitalized the Spanish-speaking business area and given rise to local Spanish-speaking periodicals, which support the maintenance of the entire Latino community. The Spanish-speaking churches have also witnessed a rise in membership. Again, the Spanish-speaking activities sponsored by churches are attended by Puerto Ricans, as well as other Latinos, and are instrumental in language maintenance.

The Latino community in Brentwood enjoys the support of a wide network of political and social groups committed to defending the interests of the Latino community. Most people leading and participating in these groups are Puerto Rican, although membership from other Latino subgroups is rising. These groups are instrumental in fighting for the rights of Latinos as was clear when the English Only referendum was proposed and when the police were found to be ignoring calls from Spanish-speaking community members.

At the social level, it is important to consider the speaking patterns of children and how these relate to language maintenance. As we have seen, young Puerto Rican children do speak Spanish in the home, especially if they are cared for by recent arrivals or older relatives. As the children grow up, they are likely to restrict Spanish language use to the home environment in contexts when they are speaking to older monolingual family and friends. In the home, the use of both Spanish and English is most common. As they mature, some Latino young people continue to speak Spanish only in restricted contexts, whereas others reactivate their passive Spanish as they interact with Spanish-dominant adults and monolingual recent arrivals. This is especially true of those young people who take jobs where they are in contact with the Latino community and/or participate in the vibrant Latino churches. As the influx of Latinos in Brentwood continues to grow, employment opportunities in which knowledge of Spanish is important also grow.

Today, everywhere in the United States, the Latino population is in a state of great flux. Predictions point to immense Hispanic population growth across the United States. What will this mean for Spanish language maintenance and change? As the numbers multiply and the political and, especially, economic clout of Latinos increases, will this have a profound effect on the social institutions of the country? Will bilingualism, which today is perceived as a threat by many mainstream Americans, become the accepted or unaccepted norm? Will the language shift and loss documented in the present research be halted and reversed?

In the quest to identify processes of language shift and language loss, very often generalizations about the demise of the entire language system are presented as foregone conclusions. Unfortunately, the very dynamic nature of bilingualism is not considered. The life cycle of language change escapes comment. The idea that teenagers who today are reluctant and uncomfortable speaking Spanish may tomorrow be motivated for multiple reasons (such as economics, relationships, and politics) to improve their Spanish is not entertained. In fact, young community members I spoke with gave many such explanations for reactivating their mostly passive Spanish. Several young Puerto Ricans have jobs at a social service agency where recent immigrants from Central America who speak no English are the most typical clients. Two participants were in romantic relationships with persons who are Spanish monolinguals. And, a group of young men had developed a fervent interest in the political status of the Puerto Rican cause both on the island and in the United States. Their understanding of U.S. cultural domination led them to reactivate their dormant Spanish.

Yet the situation is complex; this is only one side of the coin. Other young people would not agree to an interview with me in Spanish. They were not hesitant to talk to me if the conversation took place in English, but felt shy about using their Spanish for an extended conversation with someone who was not a family member. Sometimes these were young-sters whom I observed in other contexts speaking Spanish with family and monolingual friends but who felt insecure about their abilities in a different activity. Others seemed reluctant to speak Spanish under any circumstances, even in the home, although all Puerto Ricans observed in the community seemed to retain at least a passive knowledge of Spanish. Examination of these youngsters' Spanish could very well indicate a higher incidence of the incorporation of English language material than that found in my study. These youngsters were in the minority, however, and again the future of their Spanish will be deter-mined by the networks they pursue as adults.

The point is that speakers with a range of language abilities reside in the community and thus the future Spanish-speaking situation is complex and unpredictable. These speakers live in a dynamic context in which external, as well as personal, experiences can bring about dra-matic changes in linguistic habits. This is not to overlook the possibility that the Latino young people may also leave the neighborhood, move away from Spanish-speaking family and friends, and form intimate relationships with English monolinguals. For political reasons, some will see assimilation to Anglo language and culture as the path to take. Although language use and attitudes in Brentwood do not suggest hardline assimilationist tendencies in the community, the acceptance of English as the dominant language has implications at other levels as well. The study of the content of the narratives presented here suggests speakers both internalize and resist dominant ideologies about lan-guage and ethnicity. In the future, the consequences of this ambivalence may very well play themselves out in terms of language maintenance and shift.

When considering the implications of my findings on the grammatical structure of Spanish, the issue of data base and methodology are central. In other studies with similar populations of U.S. Latino speakers, greater simplification and change are noted (Gutiérrez, 1990; Ocampo, 1990; Silva-Corvalán, 1988, 1989, 1990). Why are my findings different from those of other studies of language evolution across generations using conversational data? One possibility is that most previous re-search analyzes Mexican American data, whereas I am studying a Puerto Rican community. Although these communities share many characteristics there are also differences. Most of the studies (Gutiérrez, 1990; Ocampo, 1990; Silva-Corvalán, 1988, 1989, 1990) comparable to my research are based on the Los Angeles Latino Community. This community differs from the Brentwood suburban community in several important ways. First the dynamics of city living differ from those of suburban life. The size of the communities in question and the degree of contact residents have with persons of other national groups are factors that may account for differences. Also, the economic situation of the Brentwood Latino community tends to be more stable than that of the Los Angeles community. In any case, the processes and rates of change may be different for each U.S. Latino community depending on the interaction of its unique set of external and internal variables.

Another possibility concerns my data corpus itself; unlike other studies, which use all speech data gathered in conversations, I focus exclusively on oral narratives of the past. These narratives are one of the most basic speech types that speakers can be asked to perform. Children acquire narrative skills early; even the most unsophisticated speakers can produce a basic narrative. However, when the narratives of my English-dominant group are analyzed for the complexity of both structure and content they prove to be as rich in discourse strategies, verb tenses, and clause density as the narratives of Spanish-dominant speakers.

Finally, one might ask how sociolinguistic study serves the people in the community described. At the very least, we can gain an understanding of the interaction of social and language issues. From this study we learn that, overall, the Puerto Rican community of Brentwood has very positive attitudes toward their culture and both Spanish and English. All those surveyed stress the importance of their native language in their lives. For all generations, Spanish has primarily affective value. One question that community members might ponder is whether affective factors are enough to foster maintenance of the language, given that maintenance is the expressed desire of the community. This question cannot be extracted from its particular context. In the situation studied here, a New York suburban community that continues to experience massive immigration from Spanish-speaking, primarily Central American, countries it is difficult to predict the future. As the community grows, institutions slowly, and often with resistance change to meet new demands. As we have seen, many bilingual social agencies now exist that offer educational, cultural, and social programs in Spanish. The police department, likewise, has had to make adjustments. Spanish-speaking churches with activist participants sponsor many activities in Spanish, including language classes for children and young adults. The educational system must deal with the influx of immigrant students from Central America who present an entirely unforeseen and still unmet challenge. This suburban district must now decide how to service a totally new student: a 13- or 14-year-old child who has never seen the inside of a classroom in her war-torn former home, a child who speaks not a word of English, and has never held a pencil in her fingers. The future of this particular school population seems uncertain. But should the district decide to expand its limited bilingual education program, this could have positive repercussions for language maintenance across the community.

How the Puerto Rican community continues to respond to its new Central and Latin American neighbors also remains to be seen. So far the reception has been mixed. Whereas many Puerto Ricans seek to help the new arrivals by shifting the focus of some social service agencies to meet the needs of the immigrant population, some Puerto Ricans resent them because they think the newcomers are taking away job opportunities and causing property values to decrease. If interactions and intermingling continue to occur this may aid the quest for Spanish maintenance, because both young and old Central and Latin American nationals use Spanish to a greater extent and in more contexts than the Puerto Ricans. However, as we have seen in Brentwood, as in other communities across the United States, the relationship between old and new immigrants is fraught with difficulties.

Before we can draw conclusions about Spanish in the United States, individual communities must be studied in their own contexts. One tendency of the work on Spanish in the United States has been an eagerness to generalize the findings of isolated studies to all Latino communities; but the specific sociocultural contexts that people (and languages) live in often foster very different conclusions. The results of this study indicate that the Spanish of Puerto Ricans living in Brentwood continues to survive in a restricted context. Across the population of Brentwood Puerto Ricans of all ages and language proficiencies, the Spanish language continues to assume an important practical, symbolic, and affective role.

In reviewing the studies of the Spanish spoken by second- and third-generation speakers, I wonder whether there ever will come a time when linguistic innovations, ways of speaking, and the mixing of languages are seen as resources rather than handicaps. It would be refreshing if, instead of adapting a perspective which assumes attrition, future studies on U.S. Spanish were grounded in the idea of the bilingual's creativity, and sought to document the innovative and inventive strategies Puerto Ricans and other Latinos use to express themselves in the codes of their linguistic repertoire. This study was inspired by such a desire.

Appendix

Questionnaire for Parents
(*Cuestionario para los Padres*)

Please answer the following questions (*Si prefiere contestar en español,
vea la otra cara de esta hoja*)

1. What languages do you speak?
   _____
2. What language did you learn first? English_____ Spanish_____
   Both _____
3. How old were you when you learned English?_____
   Spanish?_____
4. Can you read in Spanish?_____ In English?_____
   Both?_____
5. Can you write in Spanish?_____ In English? _____
   Both?_____
6. What language do you speak better? English_____
   Spanish_____ Both_____
7. Which language(s) (Spanish, English, Both) do you use when
   you speak with your: spouse_____ children_____
   father_____ mother_____
   brothers and sisters_____ friends_____
   work mates_____ boss_____
8. Is the Spanish you speak different from the Spanish spoken by:
   (Answer yes or no) Puerto Ricans from the island_____
   Puerto Ricans from New York_____ Dominicans_____
   Colombians_____ Central Americans_____
9. How is it different?_____
10. How would you describe good Spanish?_____
    _____
11. Do you speak it? _____
12. How would you describe good English? _____
    _____
13. Do you speak it?_____

14. Are there some things that can be said in one language but not in the other?_____
    For example:_____
    _____

15. Do you ever mix Spanish and English when you speak?_____

16. Why do you mix them?_____

17. Do you know others who mix them?_____

18. How do you feel about mixing languages? It is good_____
    It is bad_____ Other_____

19. Indicate the groups you think mix more: Puerto Ricans from the Island_____ Puerto Ricans from New York_____
    Dominicans_____ Central Americans_____

20. Do your children mix the languages? Yes_____ No_____
    Sometimes_____

21. Do you tell them not to?_____

22. Is it important for you that your children learn Spanish?_____

23. Why? _____
    _____

24. Is it important that your children learn English_____

25. Why?_____
    _____

26. Who should teach the children Spanish?
    parents_____ schools_____ both_____

**Please indicate your opinion concerning
the following statements:**

27. To be Hispanic you have to speak Spanish.
    Yes ____ No_____ Don't Know_____

28. Hispanics who don't know Spanish divide the community.
    Yes ____ No_____ Don't Know_____

29. Hispanics on Long Island have maintained their culture.
    Yes ____ No_____ Don't Know_____

30. Hispanics on Long Island have maintained Spanish.
    Yes ____ No_____ Don't Know____

31. It is important to me to speak Spanish.
    Yes ____ No_____ Don't Know____

32. Hispanic young people don't want to speak Spanish.
    Yes ____ No_____ Don't Know____

33. Hispanic young people don't know how to speak Spanish well.
    Yes ____ No_____ Don't Know_____

34. Hispanics on Long Island suffer discrimination.
    Yes ____ No_____ Don't Know____

35. Hispanics on Long Island suffer discrimination because of language problems.
    Yes ____ No ____ Don't Know ____
36. Hispanics on Long Island are united.
    Yes ____ No ____ Don't Know ____

Personal Information

37. Age____
38. Sex_____
39. Occupation_____
40. Place of birth_____
41. Town where you live_____
42. Years here_____
43. Where did you live before this town? _____
44. Why did you move to Long Island?_____
45. Years of education?_____
46. Place of education?_____
47. Father's Place of Birth?_____
48. Mother's Place of Birth?_____
49. Please check all the labels you use to define yourself or add your
    own. Hispanic_____ Hispanic American_____ Latino_____
    Puerto Rican_____ Dominican_____ Colombian_____
    Salvadoran_____ Honduran_____ Ecuadorian_____
    Nuyorican_____ American_____ Other_____
50. Your comments about anything in the survey.

References

Allport, G. (1958). *The nature of prejudice*. New York: Anchor Books.

Alvarez, C. (1988). An interpretative analysis of narration in social interaction. In Language Policy Task Force (Ed.), *Speech and ways of speaking in a bilingual Puerto Rican community* (pp. 139–183). New York: Centro de Estudios Puertorriqueños.

Alvarez, C. (1989). Code-switching in narrative performance: A Puerto Rican speech community in New York. In O. García & R. Otheguy (Eds.), *English across cultures, cultures across English* (pp. 373–386). Berlin: Mouton de Gruyten.

Andersen, R. (1982). Determining the linguistic attributes of language attrition. In R. D. Lambert & B. F. Freed (Eds.), *The loss of language skills* (pp. 83–118). Rowley, MA: Newbury House Publishers.

Anzaldúa, G. (1987). *Borderlands / La frontera*. San Francisco, CA: Spinsters/Aunt Lute Book Company.

Appel, R., & Muysken, P. (Eds.). (1987). *Language contact and bilingualism*. London: Edward Arnold.

Attinasi, J. (1979). Language attitudes in a Puerto Rican Community. In R. Padilla (Ed.), *Ethnoperspectives in bilingual education research: Bilingual education and public policy in the United States* (pp. 408–461). Ypsilanti: Eastern Michigan University.

Beaman, K. (1984). Coordination and subordination revisited: Syntactic complexity in spoken and written narrative discourse. In D. Tannen (Ed.), *Coherence in spoken and written narrative discourse* (pp. 45–80). Norwood, NJ: Ablex.

Bello, A., & Rufino C. (1958). *Gramática de la lengua castellana* [Grammar of the Castilian Language]. Buenos Aires: Editorial Sapona Argentina.

Bennet, A., & Pedraza, P. (1988). Theory and practice in the study of discourse practices, cultural formations, consciousness, and social change. In Language Policy Task Force (Ed.), *Speech and ways of speaking in a bilingual Puerto Rican community* (pp. 99–137). New York: Centro de Estudios Puertorriqueños.

Bernstein B. (1970). *Class, codes and control vol. 1: Theoretical studies toward a sociology of language*. London: Routledge & Kegan Paul.

Bills, G. (1975). Linguistic research on United States Hispanics: State of the art. In R. Teschner, G. Bills, & J. Craddock (Eds.), *Spanish and English of United States Hispanics: A critical, annotated linguistic bibliography* (pp. v–xxii). Arlington, VA: Center for Applied Linguistics.

Blake, R. (1985). From research to the classroom: Notes on the subjunctive. *Hispania, 68*, 166–173.

Blom, J., & Gumperz, J. J. (1972). Social meaning in linguistic structures: Code-switching in Norway. In J. J. Gumperz & D. Hymes (Eds.), *Directions in sociolinguistics: The ethnography of communication* (pp. 407–435). New York: Holt, Rinehart and Winston.

Bureau of the Census. (1991). *The Hispanic population in the United States. Current population reports*, (series P–20, No. 455). Washington, DC: U.S. Government Printing Office.

Cárdenas, D. (1982). Morphosyntactic preferences in the Spanish of Southern California. *Word, 33,* 29–40.

Carranza, M. (1982). Attitudinal research on Hispanic language. In E. B. Ryan & H. Giles (Eds.), *Attitudes toward language variation* (pp. 63–83). London: Edward Arnold.

Chavez, L. (1991). *Out of the barrio: Toward a new politics of Hispanic assimilation.* New York: Basic Books.

Dorian, N. (1981). *Language death: The life cycle of a Scottish Gaelic dialect.* Philadelphia: University of Pennsylvania Press.

Dvorak, T. (1983). Subject–object reversals in the use of *gustar* among New York Hispanics. In L. Elías-Olivares (Ed.), *Spanish in the U.S. setting: Beyond the Southwest* (pp. 21–36). Rosslyn, VA: National Clearinghouse for Bilingual Education.

Elías-Olivares, L. (1982). Language use in a Chicano community: A sociolinguistic approach. In P. Turner (Ed.), *Bilingualism in the Southwest* (pp. 263–279). Tucson: University of Arizona Press.

Escamilla, P. (1982). *A sociolinguistic study of modal selection among Mexican-American college students in Texas.* Unpublished PhD dissertation, The Universtiy of Texas at Austin.

Fanon, F. (1967). *Black skin white masks.* New York: Grove Press.

Fernández, R. (1990). *Actitudes hacia los cambios de códigos en Nuevo México: Reacciones de un sujeto a ejemplos de su habla* [Attitudes toward code-mixing in New Mexico: One subject's reaction to examples of his speech]. In J. Bergen (Ed.), *Spanish in the United States: Sociolinguistic issues* (pp. 49–58). Washington, DC: Georgetown University Press.

Fishman, J., Cooper, R., & Ma, R. (1971). *Bilingualism in the barrio.* Bloomington: Indiana University Press.

Flores, J., & Yudice, G. (1990). Living borders/ buscando América. *Social Text, 24,* 57–84.

Floyd, M. B. (1978). Verb usage in Southwest Spanish: A review. *The Bilingual Review / La Revista Bilingüe, 5,* 76–90.

Floyd, M. B. (1990). Sentence complexity and clause subordination in children's speech. *Hispania, 73,* 488–497.

Frey, W. (1993). *Vivan los suburbios* [The suburbs live]. *American Demographics, 15,* 30–38.

Fries, C., & Pike, K. (1949). Coexistent phonemic systems. *Language, 25,* 29–50.

Gal, S. (1979). *Language shift: Social determinants of language change in bilingual Austria.* London: Academic Press.

García, M. E., & Terrell, T. (1977). Is the use of mood in Spanish subject to variable constraints? In M. P. Hagiwari (Ed.), *Studies in romance linguistics: Proceedings of the fifth symposium on romance linguistics* (pp. 214–226). Rowley, MA: Newbury House.

García, O., Evangelista, I., Martínez, M., Disla, C., & Bonifacio, P. (1988). Spanish language use and attitudes: A study of two New York City communities. *Language in Society, 17,* 475–511.

Giles, H., Bourhis, R., & Taylor, D. (1979). Toward a theory of language in ethnic group relations. In H. Giles (Ed.), *Language, ethnicity and intergroup relations* (pp. 307–348). London: Academic Press.

Gili Gaya, S. (1968). *Curso superior de sintaxis española* [An advanced course of Spanish syntax]. Barcelona, España: Talleres Gráficos de Bilbiograf, S.A.

Gray, C. (1989). Loud "no gracias" for proposal to make English the official country language. *Newsday,* 4 March, p. 5.

Grosjean, F. (1982). *Life with two languages.* Boston, MA: Harvard University Press.

Guanil, E. (1980). The Puerto Ricans in Brentwood. In S. La Gumina (Ed.), *Ethnicity in suburbia: The Long Island experience* (pp. 37–42). Nassau, NY: Nassau Community College.

Gutiérrez, M. (1990). *Sobre el mantenimiento de las cláusulas subordinadas en el español de Los Angeles* [On the maintenance of subordinate clauses in the Spanish of Los Angeles]. In J. Bergen (Ed.), *Spanish in the United States: Sociolinguistic issues* (pp. 31–39). Washington, DC: Georgetown University Press.

Hamers, J. F., & Blanc, M. H. A. (1990). *Bilinguality & bilingualism*. Cambridge, England: Cambridge University Press.

Hart-González, L. (1985). Pan-Hispanism and subcommunity in Washington, D.C. In L. Elías Olivares, E. A. Leone, R. Cisneros, & J. R. Gutiérrez (Eds.), *Spanish language use and public life in the United States* (pp. 73–88). Berlin: Mouton Publishers.

Hart-González, L. & Feingold, M. (1990). Retention of Spanish in the home. *International Journal of the Sociology of Language, 84*, 5–34.

Haugen, E. (1950). The analysis of linguistic borrowing. *Language, 26*, 210–231.

Haugen, E. (1969). *The Norwegian language in America*. Bloomington: Indiana University Press.

Heller, M. (Ed.). (1988). *Codeswitching*. New York: Mouton de Gruyter.

Hill, J. (1973). Subordinate clause density and language function. In C. Corum, T. Smith-Stark, & A. Weiser (Eds.), *You take the high node and I'll take the low node: Papers from a comparative syntax festival* (pp. 33–52). Chicago, IL: Chicago Linguistics Society.

Holmes, J. (1986). Functions of you know in women's and men's speech. *Language and society, 15*, 1–22.

hooks, b. (1984). *Feminist theory: From margin to center*. Boston, MA: South End Press.

hooks, b. (1993). Seduced by violence no more. In E. Buchwald, P. R. Fletcher, & M. Roth (Eds.), *Transforming a rape culture* (pp. 351–356). Minneapolis: Milkweed Editions.

Hooper, J., & Terrell, T. (1974). A semantic based analysis of mood in Spanish. *Hispania, 57*, 484–494.

Hudson-Edwards, A., & Bills, G. D. (1980). Intergenerational language shift in an Albuquerque barrio. In E. L. Blansitt, Jr. & R. V. Teschner (Eds.), *A festschrift for Jacob Ornstein* (pp. 139–156). Rowley, MA: Newbury House Publishers.

Hutchington, R. (1990, October). *Language patterns among Hispanic groups in Chicago*. Paper presented at the Spanish in U.S. Conference, Chicago, IL.

Hyltenstam, K., & Viberg, A. (1993). Linguistic progression and regression an introduction. In K. Hyltenstam & A. Viberg (Eds.), *Progression & regression in language* (pp. 3–36). Cambridge, England: Cambridge University Press.

Kachru, B. (1983). *The Indianization of English: The English language in India*. Oxford: Pergamon Press.

Kachru, B. (1985). The bilingual's creativity. In R. Kaplan (Ed.), *Annual review of applied linguistics* (pp. 20–33). Cambridge, England: Cambridge University Press.

Kachru, B. (1986). *The alchemy of English*. Oxford: Pergamon Press.

Kalman, I. (1985). Are there really no primative languages? In D. O. Olson, N. Torrance, & A. Hildyards (Eds.), *Literacy, language, and learning* (pp. 148–166). Cambridge: Cambridge University Press.

Klein, F. (1980). A quanititative study of syntactic and pragmatic indicators of change in the Spanish of bilinguals in the U.S. In W. Labov, (Ed.), *Locating language in time and space* (pp. 69–82). New York: Academic Press.

Klein, F. (1986). *La cuestión del anglicismo: Apriorismos y métodos* [The question of Anglicisms: Apriorisms and methods]. *Thesaurus, Boletín del Instituto Caro y Cuervo, XL*, 1–16.

Klein, P. (1977). Semantic factors in Spanish mood. *Glossa, 11*, 3–19.

Knoll, B. (1977). Combining ideas in written and spoken English: A look at subordination and coordination. In E. Keenan & T. Bennet (Eds.), *Discourse across time and space*. Los Angeles: University of Southern California.

Koike, D. A. (1987). Code switching in the bilingual Chicano narrative. *Hispania, 70*, 148–54.

Labov, W. (1972). The transformation of experience in narrative syntax. In *Language in the inner city* (pp. 354–396). Philadelphia: University of Pennsylvania Press.

Labov, W., & Waletzky, J. (1967). Narrative analysis: Oral versions of personal experience. In J. Helm (Ed.), *Essays on the verbal and visual arts* (pp. 12–44). Seattle: University of Washington Press.

Lambert, R. D., & Freed, B. F. (Eds.). (1982). *The loss of language skills.* Rowley: Newbury House Publishers.

Language Policy Task Force. (1978). Language policy and the Puerto Rican community. *The Bilingual Review / Revista Bilingüe, 1,* 1–40.

Language Policy Task Force. (1980). Rethinking diglossia. (Centro de Estudios Puertorriqueños. Working Paper # 9). New York: City University of New York.

Language Policy Task Force. (1982). *Intergenerational perspectives on bilingualism: From community to classroom.* New York: City University of New York.

Lantolf, J. (1978). The variable constraints on mood in Puerto Rican Spanish. In M. Suner (Ed.), *Contemporary studies in romance linguistics* (pp. 193–217). Washington, DC: Georgetown University Press.

Lantolf, J. (1983). Toward a comparative dialectology of U.S. Spanish. In L. Elías Olivares (Ed.), *Spanish in the U.S. setting: Beyond the Southwest* (pp. 3–20). Rosslyn, VA: National Clearinghouse for Bilingual Education.

Lavandera, B. (1983). Shifting moods in Spanish discourse. In F. Klein (Ed.), *Discourse perspectives on syntax* (pp. 209–236). New York: Academic Press.

Lavandera, B. (1981). Lo quebramos, but only in performance. In R. Durán (Ed.). *Latino language and communicative behavior* (pp. 49–67). Norwood, NJ: Ablex.

Lavandera, B. (1984). *Variación y significado* [Variation and meaning]. Buenos Aires: Hachette.

Linde, C. (1993). *Life stories: The creation of coherence.* New York: Oxford University Press.

Long Island Regional Planning Board. (1981). *Population 1980, Race and Spanish origin, report.*

Lope Blanch, J. (1983). *Análisis gramatical del discurso* [Grammatical analysis of discourse]. Ciudad de México: Universidad Nacional Autónoma de México.

Lope Blanch, J. (1990). *La estructura del discurso en el habla de Mora, Nuevo México* [Structure of discourse in the speech of Mora, New Mexico]. *Romance Philology, 1,* 26–35.

Matsuda, M. J. (1993). Public response to racist speech: Considering the victim's story. In M. J. Matsuda, C. R. Lawrence, III, R. Delgado, & K. W. Crenshaw (Eds.), *Words that wound: Critical race theory, assaultive speech, and the first amendment* (pp. 17–52). Boulder, CO: Westview Press.

Moraga, C. (1983). *Loving in the war years.* Boston, MA: South End Press.

Mougeon, R., Beniak, E., & Valois, D. (1985). *Issues in the study of language contact: Evidence from Ontarian French.* Toronto: Centre for Franco-Ontarian Studies.

Ocampo, F. (1990). *El subjuntivo en tres generaciones de hablantes bilingües* [The subjunctive in three generations of bilingual speakers]. In J. Bergen (Ed.), *Spanish in the United States: Sociolinguistic issues* (pp. 39–48). Washington, DC: Georgetown University Press.

Ochs, E. (1979). Planned and unplanned discourse. In T. Givón (Ed.), *Discourse and syntax* (pp. 51–80). New York: Academic Press.

Olojede, D. (1991). A police primer on Spanish. *Newsday,* 14 August, p. 4.

Otheguy, R., & García, O. (1988). Diffusion of lexical innovations in the Spanish of Cuban Americans. In J. Ornstein-Galicia, G. Green, & D. J. Bixler-Marquez (Eds.), *Research and issues and problems in U.S. Spanish* (pp. 203–237). El Paso: Pan American University at Brownsville in cooperation with University of Texas at El Paso.

Padilla, F. (1985). *Latino ethnic consciousness*. Notre Dame: University of Notre Dame Press.

Patella, V., & Kuvelsky, W. (1973). Situational variations in language patterns. *Social Science Quarterly, 53*, 855–864.

Pedraza, P. (1985). Language maintenance among Puerto Ricans. In L. Elías-Olivares, E. A. Leone, R. Cisneros, & J. R. Gutiérrez (Eds.), *Spanish language use and public life in the United States* (pp. 59–72). Berlin: Mouton de Gruyter.

Pedraza, P. (1987). *An ethnographic analysis of language use in the Puerto Rican community of East Harlem*. (Centro de estudios puertorriqueños working paper series). New York: City University of New York.

Pellicer, D. (1992). Storytelling in Mazahua Spanish. *International Journal of the Sociology of Language, 96*, 71–88.

Polanyi, L. (1985). *Telling the American story: A structural and cultural analysis of conversational storytelling*. Norwood, NJ: Ablex.

Poplack, S. (1982a). Bilingualism and the vernacular. In B. Hartford, A. Valdman, & C. Foster (Eds.), *Issues in international bilingual education* (pp. 1–23). New York: Plenum Press.

Poplack, S. (1982b). "Sometimes I'll start a sentence in Spanish y *termino en español.*" In J. Amastae & L. Elías-Olivares (Eds.), *Spanish in the United States: Sociolinguistic aspects* (pp. 230–263). Cambridge, England: Cambridge University Press.

Poplack, S. (1983). Bilingual competence: Linguistic interference or grammatical integrity? In L. Elías-Olivares (Ed.), *Spanish in the U.S.: Beyond the southwest* (pp. 111–125). Rosslyn, VA: National Clearinghouse for Bilingual Education.

Poplack, S. (1985). Contrasting patterns of code-switching in two communities. In H. Warkentyne (Ed.), *Papers from the V international conference on methods in dialectology* (pp. 365–385). University of Victoria: Department of Linguistics.

Poplack, S., & Sankoff, D. (1984). Borrowing: The synchrony of integration. *Linguistics, 22*, 99–135.

Poplack, S., & Sankoff, D., & Miller, C. (1988). The social correlates and linguistic processes of lexical borrowing and assimilation. *Linguistics, 26*, 47–104.

Poplack, S., & Sankoff, D., & Pousada, A. (1982). Competing influences on gender assignment: Variable process, stable outcome. *Lingua, 57*, 1–28.

Pousada, A., & Poplack, S. (1981). No case for convergence: The Puerto Rican verb system in a language contact situation. In G. Keller & J. Fishman (Eds.), *Bilingual education for Hispanic students in the United States* (pp. 207–237). New York: Teachers College Press.

Ramsey, M. M. (1956). *A textbook of modern Spanish* (Rev. ed.). New York: Holt, Rinehart and Winston.

Rich, A. (1983). Compulsory heterosexuality and lesbian existence. In A. Snitow, C. Stansell, & S. Thompson (Eds.) *Powers of desire: The politics of sexuality* (pp. 177–205). New York: Monthly Review Press.

Rickford, J. (1986). The need for new approaches to social class analysis in sociolinguistics. *Language and Communication, 6*, 215–21.

Rickford, J. (1987). The haves and the have nots: sociolinguistic surveys and the assessment of speaker competence. *Language and Society, 16*, 149–177.

Riessman, C. K. (1987). When gender is not enough: Women interviewing women. *Gender & Society, 1*, 172–207.

Riessman, C. K. (1988). Words of difference: Contrasting experience in marriage and narrative style. In A. Todd & S. Fisher (Eds.), *Power and discourse: The power of talk* (pp. 151–173). Norwood, NJ: Ablex Publishing Corporation.

Romaine, S. (1982). What is a speech community? In S. Romaine (Ed.), *Sociolinguistic variation in speech communities* (pp. 13–25). London: Edward Arnold.

Romaine, S. (1984). *The language of children and adolescence*. Oxford: Blackwell.

Rosenberg, T. J. (1981). *A profile of Hispanic households in Suffolk County New York, 1980*. Unpublished manuscript.

Ruskin, F., & Varenne, H. (1983). The production of ethnic discourse: American and Puerto Rican patterns. In J. Bain (Ed.), *The sociogenesis of language and human conduct* (pp. 553–568). New York: Plenum Press.

Salah, G. (1990). Discourse analysis and embedding depth of utterances: Clause analysis technique as a measure of complexity. In L. A. Arena (Ed.), *Language proficiency* (pp. 121–128). New York: Plenum Press.

Sánchez, R. (1983). *Chicano discourse*. Rowley, MA: Newbury House.

Schiffrin, D. (1981). Tense variation in narrative. *Language, 57*, 45–67.

Schiffrin, D. (1987). *Discourse markers*. Cambridge, England: Cambridge University Press.

Schleppegrell, M. (1991). Subordination and linguistic complexity. *Discourse Processes*, 117–131.

Seliger, H. W., & Vago, R. M. (Eds). (1991). *First language attrition*. Cambridge, England: Cambridge University Press.

Silberstein, S. (1988). Ideology as process: Gender ideology in courtship narratives. In A. Todd & S. Fisher (Eds.), *Power and discourse: The power of talk* (pp.125–149). Norwood, NJ: Ablex.

Silva-Corvalán, C. (1983a). Code-shifting patterns in Chicano Spanish. In L. Elías-Olivares (Ed.), *Spanish in the U.S.: Beyond the southwest* (pp. 79–88). Rossyln, VA: National Clearing House for Bilingual Education.

Silva-Corvalán, C. (1983b). Tense and aspect in oral Spanish narrative: context and meaning. *Language, 59*, 760–779.

Silva-Corvalán, C. (1984). The social profile of a syntactic-semantic variable: Three verb forms in Old Castile. *Hispania, 67*, 594–601.

Silva-Corvalán, C. (1986). Bilingualism and language contact. *Language, 62*, 587–608.

Silva-Corvalán, C. (1988). Oral narrative along the Spanish–English bilingual continuum. In J. Staczek (Ed.), *On Spanish, Portuguese, Catalan linguistics* (pp. 172–184). Washington, DC: Georgetown University Press.

Silva-Corvalán, C. (1989). Past and present perspectives on language change in U.S. Spanish. *International Journal of the Sociology of Language, 79*, 53–66.

Silva-Corvalán, C. (1990). Current issues in studies of language contact. *Hispania, 73*, 162–176.

Sílva-Corvalán, C. (1994). *Language contact and change: Spanish in Los Angeles*. Oxford, England: Oxford University Press.

Solé, Y. (1977). Continuidad/descontinuidad idiomática en el español tejano [Idiomatic continuity/discontinuity in Texan Spanish]. *The Bilingual Review / La Revista Bilingüe, 4*, 189–199.

Solé, Y. (1978). Sociocultural and sociopsychological factors in differential language retentiveness by sex. *International Journal of the Sociology of Language, 17*, 29–44.

Solé, Y. (1990). Bilingualism: Stable or transitional? The case of Spanish in the United States. *International Journal of the Sociology of Language, 84*, 5–34.

Solé, Y., & Solé, C. (1977). *A modern Spanish syntax: A study in contrast*. Lexington, MA: D.C. Heath.

Somos Uno. (1989, April). *Report of statement made on April 24, 1989 before the members of the Puerto Rican and Hispanic Legislative Task Force*, Albany, NY.

Sridhar, S. N. (1978). On the functions of code-mixing in Kannada. *International Journal of Sociology of Language, 16*, 109–117.

Tannen, D. (1979). What's in a frame? In R. Freedle (Ed.), *New directions in discourse processing* (pp. 137–181). Norwood, NJ: Ablex.

Tannen, D. (1989). *Talking voices: repetition, dialogue, and imagery in conversational discourse*. Cambridge, England: Cambridge University Press.

Teschner, R., Bills, G., & Craddock, J. (Eds.). (1975). *Spanish and English of the United States Hispanos: A critical, annotated, linguistic bibliography*. Arlington, VA: Center for Applied Linguistics.

Thompson, S. A. (1987). "Subordination" and narrative event structure. In R. Tomlin (Ed.), *Coherence and grounding in discourse* (pp. 435–454). Amsterdam: John Benjamins.

Torres, L. (1988). *Linguistic change in a language contact situation: A cross-generational study*. Unpublished doctoral dissertation, University of Illinois at Urbana-Champaign.

Torres, L. (1989). Code-mixing and borrowing in a New York Puerto Rican community: a cross-generational study. *World Englishes, 8*, 419–432.

Torres, L. (1990a). Mood selection among New York Puerto Ricans. *International Journal of Sociology of Language, 79*, 67–79.

Torres, L. (1990b). Spanish in the United States: The struggle for legitimacy. In J. Bergen (Ed.), *Spanish in the United States: Sociolinguistic issues* (pp. 142–151). Washington, DC: Georgetown University Press.

Torres, L. (1991). The study of U.S. Spanish varieties: Some theoretical and methodological issues. In C. Klee & L. A. Ramos (Eds.), *Sociolinguistics of the Spanish-speaking world: Iberia, Latin America, United States* (pp. 255–270). Tempe, AZ: Bilingual Press/Editorial Bilingüe.

Torres, L. (1992a). Code-mixing as a narrative strategy in the Puerto Rican community. *World Englishes, 11*, 183–194.

Torres, L. (1992b). Women's narratives in a New York Puerto Rican community. In L. F. Rakow, (Ed.), *Women making meaning* (pp. 244–263). London: Routledge, Chapman and Hall, Inc.

Valdés, G. (1976). Social interaction and code-switching patterns: A case study of Spanish/English alternation. In G. Keller, R. Teschner, & S. Viera, *Bilingualism in the bicentennial and beyond* (pp. 53–85). New York: Bilingual Press.

Van Dijk, T. (1984). *Prejudice and discourse: An analysis of ethnic prejudice in cognition and conversation*. Amsterdam: John Benjamins.

Van Dijk, T. (1987). *Communicating racism, ethnic prejudice in thought and talk*. Newbury Park, CA: Sage.

Van Dijk, T. (1993). Stories and racism. In D. K. Mumby (Ed.), *Narrative and social control: Critical perspectives* (pp. 121–142). Newbury Park, CA: Sage Publications.

Veltman, C. (1983). *Language shift in the United States*. Berlin: Mouton de Gruyter.

Weinreich, U. (1953). *Languages in contact*. The Hague: Mouton de Gruyter.

Weltens, B., de Bot, K., & van Els, T. (Eds.). (1986) *Language attrition in progress*. Holland: Foris Publications.

Wodak, R. (1981). Women relate, men report: Sex differences in language behavior in a therapeutic group. *Journal of Pragmatics, 5*, 261–285.

Wolfson, J. (1991) Who's in the schools, district by district. *Newsday,* 24 March, p. 5.

Wolfson, N. (1982). *The conversational historical present in American English narrative*. Dordrecht: Foris Publication.

Yamato, G. (1990). Something about the subject makes it hard to name. In G. Anzaldúa (Ed.), *Making face, making soul, haciendo caras* (pp. 20–24). San Francisco: Aunt Lute Foundation Books.

Zentella, A. C. (1985). The fate of Spanish in the United States: The Puerto Rican experience. In N. Wolfson & J. Manes (Eds.), *Language of inequality* (pp. 41–59). Berlin: Mouton de Gruyter.

Zentella, A. C. (1987). Language and female identity in the Puerto Rican community. In J. Penfield (Ed.), *Women and language in transition* (pp. 134–150). Albany, NY: State University of New York Press.

Author Index

Subject Index